Other books by Jonathan Wills

Environment and natural history:

The Dutchmen of Noss – an ornithological expedition to Shetland in 1970. Amazon, 2023.

Seabirds and Seals – the stories behind 25 years of wildlife cruises around the Shetland islands of Bressay and Noss. The Shetland Times Ltd, 2019.

Innocent Passage - the Wreck of the Tanker Braer. With Karen Warner. Mainstream, Edinburgh, 1993.

A *Place in the Sun - Shetland and Oil.* Mainstream, Edinburgh, and ISER Books, St Johns, Newfoundland, 1991.

Biography:

Sixty North to Sixty South – the lives of Jessie and Tammie Laurenson. Amazon, 2022.

Bobby the Birdman – An Anthology Celebrating the Life and Work of Bobby Tulloch. Editor and contributor, with Mike McDonnell. Birlinn, Edinburgh, 2019.

Memoirs, journalism and photography:

That Spring in Prague – a photographic memoir from 1968 (English/Czech edition). Amazon, 2023.

Reporter on the Rocks – memoirs of a recovering journalist. Amazon, 2021.

Old Rock – Shetland in pictures. Shetland Times Ltd, 1990.

Books for children:

The Travels of Magnus Pole. Amazon, 2022 (third edition, first published in 1974 by Canongate).

Magnus Pole Goes West. Amazon, 2022.

Granny Linda and the Lighthouse. Shetland Heritage Publications, 2014 (revised edition, first published in 1976 by Canongate).

Cheer Up, Grampa Gloomifjord! Illustrated by Martin Emslie. Shetland Times Ltd, 2011.

Wilma Widdershins and the Muckle Tree. Illustrated by Gurli Feilberg. Shetland Times Ltd, 2008.

Copyright Notice

To Beijing after Nixon - a grand tour of China in 1972
by Jonathan Wills

In affectionate and respectful memory of Harry Dickinson and Radha Sinha

To Beijing after Nixon

a grand tour of China in 1972

Jonathan Wills

Contents

Acknowledgements

My wife, Lesley Roberts, has patiently endured long evenings when we were supposed to be exploring the sunlit uplands of retirement but instead I was hunched over a word processor, cursing whoever it was who invented the Word program that kept crashing. Lesley is a very pernickety proof reader, thankfully, and her honest criticism was always invaluable, even if I sometimes didn't acknowledge that at the time. Any remaining typographical errors and grammatical infelicities are my own unaided work.

For the correct modern spellings of Chinese place names and personal names I have relied upon advice from the Scotland-China Association (SCA). The views expressed in this book are my own and do not necessarily reflect the opinions of the SCA or any of its members.

For help in tracing copies of Harry Dickinson's report, *Rural China*, for the World Council of Churches in 1972 I am indebted to: Harry's son Adam, who painstakingly scanned the original; and also to Professor Robin Williams, Director of the Institute for the Study of Science, Technology and Innovation at the University of Edinburgh; Dr Ewen Macpherson, Harry Dickinson's former student and his successor as a lecturer in the School of Engineering Sciences, University of Edinburgh; and to Danielle Howarth and colleagues of the Centre for Research Collections at the university's main library.

Adam Dickinson generously shared some of his late father's other papers on China. He and his sister Ellen kindly agreed to my including their father's 1972 report as an appendix to this work.

George Wallington, the Word magician, came to the rescue again and then yet again, saving my draft text when it appeared to have disintegrated and/or disappeared.

Map of China

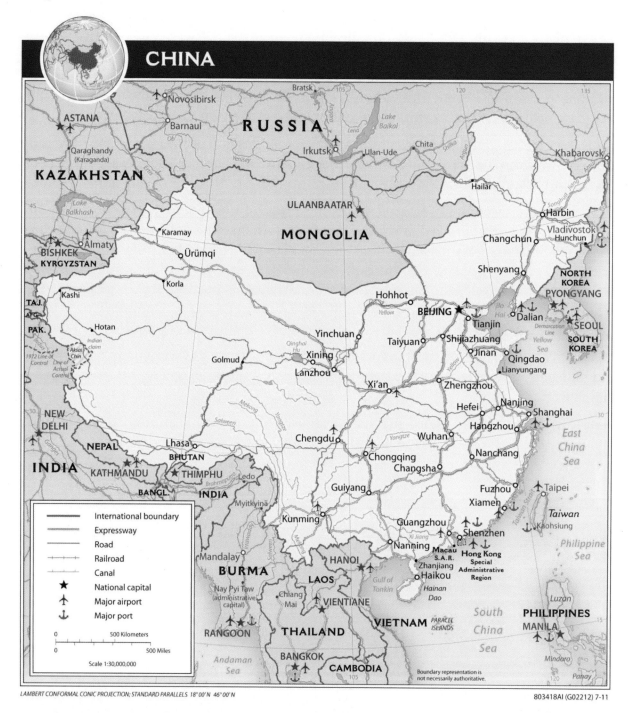

A modern map of China's main transport routes (by the CIA).

Map of the Scotland-China Association tour in 1972

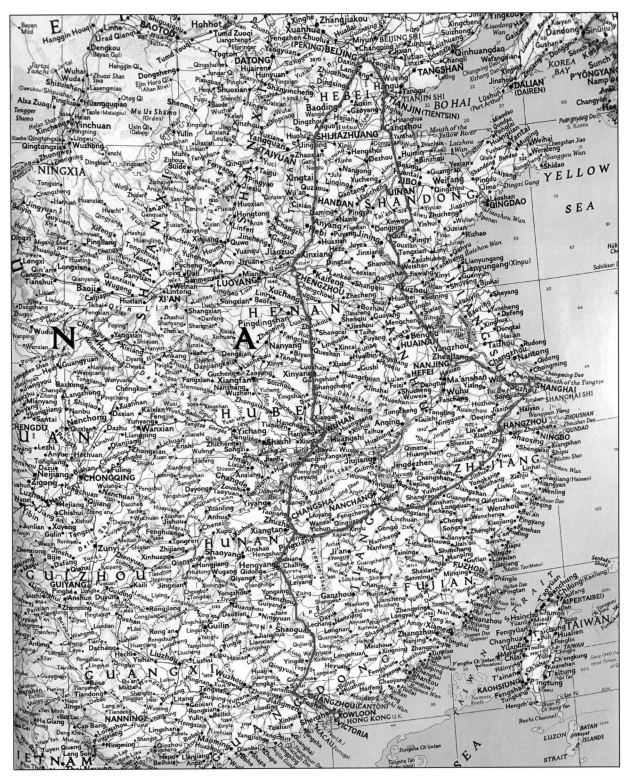

The 3,000-mile route of the Scotland-China Association's study tour, by train, from 31st August to 25th September 1972: Hong Kong – Guangzhou – Zhengzhou – Beijing – Nanjing – Wuxi – Shanghai – Guangzhou - Hong Kong.

Preface

I know, I really should have written this book about my study tour of China as soon as I got home, 51 years ago. But I was busy with other things and also, as the late Chinese Premier Zhou Enlai said when asked for his opinion on the French Revolution, it was too soon to judge. Now it may be too late. Although I never returned to China, friends who did have encouraged me to write captions to the 200 or more photographs that I took and to consult my contemporaneous notes, which somehow survived half a century in various attics.

September 1972 was a turning point, as we know now but didn't then: the Cultural Revolution's peak terror had just passed; Mao Zedong's chosen successor, Lin Biao, had died in a plane crash, fleeing after an apparent coup attempt; the People's Liberation Army had returned to barracks the previous month, after years of virtual martial law, keeping Mao's Red Guards in check; 'continuous revolution' was less popular than ever; Chinese Communist Party leaders were split between Maoist lickspittles and more reasonable communists smeared as 'capitalist roaders'; and there were the beginnings of the more relaxed, albeit still dictatorial, regime that would emerge after Mao's death in 1976. The people's communes which we were exhorted to admire (and to some extent did), turned out to be remarkably short-lived: just ten years after my trip those beacons to a glorious communist future had mostly been closed down, for sound practical reasons as much as changing ideology.

I've remained fascinated by China but my knowledge of that vast country since 1972 has been gained mainly from books, in particular startling new biographies of Mao that exposed his numerous follies, lies and murderous tyranny. The truth about the anti-Japanese war, the Chinese civil war, Mao's great famine, the Cultural Revolution – and the complicity in Mao's crimes of Deng Xiaoping, Zhou Enlai, Liu Shaoqi, Lin Biao and other Communist Party villains – has only emerged slowly, some of it quite recently. Books by Frank Dikötter, Yung Chang, Zhisui Li, Jasper Becker and the extremely brave Yang Jisheng have helped me to understand what I saw all those years ago. These writers' attempts at an honest history of modern China are now, of course, being undermined, criticised and often banned, as yet another lying emperor fabricates history to cement total power over twice as many people as lived under the Emperor Mao's evil dictatorship. Despite my reading I am still fairly ignorant but, unlike a visiting Chinese university student whom I met in the UK not long ago, I do at least know who Sun Yat Sen was and why he matters. She had never heard of him. But it was not her fault. She had been fed a dishonest draft of history.

This little book may be an insignificant footnote, merely a collection of nostalgic snapshots, but if it encourages the reader to consult more reliable and knowledgeable sources about the world's most populous country, then it will have served a purpose.

Jonathan Wills
Bressay
Shetland
May 2023

Editorial note

When I was a student I bought a large and very beautiful book that I could not really afford: *China* by the Swiss photographer Emil Schulthess[1] who in 1964 was allowed to travel throughout China. His work so inspired me that when I went to China myself, on the other side of the Cultural Revolution, my idea was to turn my colour slides into a coffee table picture book in similar style. But my snaps were not of the professional quality and high resolution required. When I pulled them out of the filing cabinet 50 years later and tried to write captions I realised the extent of my ignorance. A year or so's background reading was required before attempting the linking text. This has ballooned into the rambling narrative that lies before you.

It was tempting to divide this work into thematic sections but in the end I decided to retrace our 26-day study tour through China day by day, just as it happened. This means that some topics pop up more than once and not always in logical order. But that is how it was at the time and so I think it best to leave the storyline chronological. Fortunately, my contemporary notes are all dated and so are the faded labels on my slides in their original cardboard mounts, now rather fragile.

I was only the note-taker and photographer; the official report for the World Council of Churches was written by Harry Dickinson, with statistical help from Professor Radha Sinha. A facsimile of Harry's report[2] is included as an Appendix, divided into thematic sections (in logical order). The narrative and statistical data are still of great interest, even if one may disagree with some of Harry's conclusions.

---

[1] Schulthess, E. 1966. *China*. Collins, London and Artemis Verlags, Zurich.

[2] Dickinson, H. 1972. *Rural China 1972: a Report prepared for the Commission on the Churches' Participation in Development*. World Council of Churches, Geneva. A copy of this now very rare document is in the papers of the late Professor C. H. Waddington, held in the archives of the University of Edinburgh Library, to whose kind and diligent staff I am indebted for sight of it, having mislaid my own copy many years ago. JW. https://archives.collections.ed.ac.uk/repositories/2/archival_objects/15363

Tricky Dicky blazes a trail

The famous Mao/Nixon handshake on screen at an exhibition in Beijing. Photo: Wikipedia.

When the 37th President of the United States, Richard Milhous Nixon, resigned on 9th August 1974, his administration was mired in scandal and disgrace. Nixon's reputation has never recovered. He's still remembered as 'Tricky Dicky' because of the chicanery and political dirty tricks that brought him down after the 'Watergate' affair, when he tried and failed to cover up a robbery committed by Republican Party agents on 17th June 1972 at the Democratic Party's Washington D.C. offices, during his (successful) re-election campaign. But for Watergate, and the illegal carpet bombing of Cambodia in 1970-71, Nixon might now be much more fondly remembered. He was not a pleasant character but his two major political achievements in office do deserve credit: the ending of American involvement in the Vietnam War in 1972; and the start of rapprochement with China that same year.

For 25 years there had been no official contact (in public, at least) between the US and China so there was widespread astonishment when Nixon went on television on 15th July 1971 to announce that he would be visiting Beijing the following year. The President's and First Lady's trip to China in February 1972 was billed in American news media as 'a week that changed the world' and it is indeed doubtful whether any other foreign trip by a US President had anything like the same momentous consequences, at least before the Reagan/Gorbachev meeting in Reykjavik in 1984. Nixon and his Secretary of State Henry Kissinger's talks with Chinese Communist Party Chairman Mao Zedong and Premier Zhou Enlai started a process that eventually led to full diplomatic and commercial relations, achieving Nixon's aim of preventing a renewal of China's previous alliance with (and technical reliance upon) the Soviet Union. That had ended in 1960 after the Soviet leadership began to renounce Stalinism and adopt a policy of peaceful co-existence with the West. Mao, posing as the champion of the Third World, positively welcomed military conflicts in Latin America, Africa and Asia and regularly made hostile comments about NATO and Warsaw Pact countries. Significantly, the USSR concluded important agreements with the USA within months of 'Tricky Dicky' and Mao apparently agreeing

that same policy of peaceful co-existence. The President's meeting with Mao and Zhou Enlai in Beijing on 22nd February 1972, the after day the presidential Boeing 707, *Spirit of '76*, landed in Shanghai, also seemed to imply, without actually saying so, that China was prepared to shelve the Taiwan dispute, at least for the time being (which turned out to be half a century). The Chinese were even more adept than the serpentine Kissinger at 'smoke and mirrors' diplomacy and speech with forked tongue.

Mao had several reasons for opening his door to the Americans: he wanted to show the USSR and other states that he was a major player on the world stage who could deal independently with the USA; he wanted Taiwan's seat at the United Nations and a Chinese veto in the UN Security Council (both of which he'd got in October 1971, shortly after Kissinger's secret visit to Beijing to set up the Nixon trip); but above all he wanted covert American help to evade trade embargos designed to stop China buying advanced Western technology, particularly the equipment and skills needed to develop intercontinental ballistic missiles, long-range nuclear bombers and nuclear submarines.

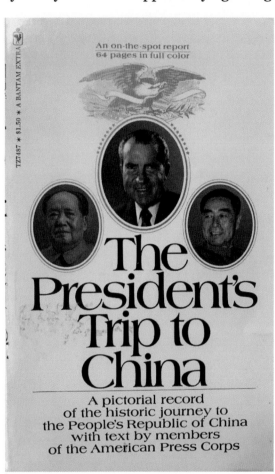

The 'instant book' on Tricky Dicky's trip.

In this (publicly unstated) aim Mao was unsuccessful. It would be many years before China acquired reliable missiles to deliver the atomic and nuclear weapons it had developed with Soviet help in the late 1950s. As Jung Chang[3] and other authors have shown, Mao was obsessed with making China a nuclear power. He contemplated world domination and to achieve it he was prepared to sacrifice millions of Chinese and other lives in a nuclear exchange. He said so repeatedly to his courtiers and occasionally in public. To pay for weapons of mass destruction he was willing to export large amounts of grain and other produce to earn foreign currency, in effect stealing food from the millions

---

[3] Jung, C. and Halliday, J. 2005, *Mao, the Unknown Story*. Jonathan Cape, London.

of peasants who suffered Mao's cruel and maniacal despotism during his 27-year reign as emperor. This pattern of callous indifference to the fate of his subjects had been apparent as early as the 1920s, when rural areas controlled by Mao's Red Army were routinely pillaged and left to starve.

Nixon's visit was largely symbolic. It made a great news media event but the USA did not sign formal agreements with China until some years later. Nonetheless it is often linked to longer term changes in China's society and economy. During the past 50 years the 'great, glorious and correct' Chinese Communist Party has retained dictatorial power, often literally 'at the barrel of a gun' (as Mao put it in the 'Little Red Book' of his sayings that his lackey Lin Biao compiled for him) but the 'capitalist roaders' so excoriated by Mao and his fellow gangsters would eventually triumph over Mao's failed experiments in state communism. Communism mutated into 'Socialism with Chinese characteristics' – partly state-owned and always state-regulated capitalism, accompanied by massive migration from the countryside to China's burgeoning cities. China, colonised and then isolated for so long, has developed into the global commercial and industrial power we know today, while the US has become its customer (and debtor) on an equally massive scale. Nixon's trip, by opening the US market to Chinese goods, is seen by many as the start of that process, which may be why his name is not universally revered in American ultra-nationalist and isolationist circles today. This should not surprise us for, like the withdrawal from Vietnam, his overtures to China came as a big and unwelcome surprise to the militant right wing of American imperialism back in 1972, and were also seen (correctly) as a betrayal of Taiwan.

Following Nixon's much-publicised visit (which received rosy-tinted coverage in American news media[4]) and talks about establishing diplomatic relations with the United Kingdom as well as the USA, the Chinese authorities began to issue tourist visas as rarely before, partly to gain favourable publicity for the purported achievements of Chairman Mao's ongoing Cultural Revolution and partly to earn much-needed foreign currency. One of the many study tours to arrive in Beijing later that year was organised by the Scotland-China Association (SCA), an independent cultural and academic organisation rather than a Maoist propaganda mouthpiece. The leading light in the SCA, and the leader of the September 1972 tour, was John Chinnery, Head of the Chinese Department at Edinburgh University, who'd founded the Scottish association in 1965-6, after disagreements within the Britain-China Friendship Association (BCFA).[5]

---

[4] For examples of this sometimes breathless coverage, see: Wilson, R. ed. (1972) *The President's Trip to China*. Bantam Books, New York.

[5] As Chinnery explained in his 1996 article for the journal *Sine*:

'The disbandment of the BCFA was a result of the Sino-Soviet split of that period. Although its policy was to welcome all who shared its aim of developing friendship with China, no matter what their political persuasion, its leadership was still strongly under the influence of the Communist Party of Great Britain. When the Chinese government expected it to side with China against Russia, the BCFA refused. This decision split the organisation, and those who disagreed with it decided to set up their own successor organisation, the Society for Anglo-Chinese Understanding (SACU). Some Scottish members of the BCFA had long desired to establish their own links with China and, perhaps goaded by

John Chinnery had first visited China in 1954 on a cultural delegation and from then on, although never an apologist for Mao's excesses, he made it his mission to help the outside world to understand the Chinese people and the communist revolution[6]. He returned in 1957 to spend a year at Beijing University, working on his Ph. D. thesis and tutoring students in modern Chinese literature. Later, he jointly edited some of Mao's letters and talks for publication. In short, he knew the country better than most westerners and was an ideal person to head up the SCA's first expedition to the Forbidden City. The arrangements he'd made, and the esteem in which he was held by Chinese academics and officials, ensured that the visitors from Scotland enjoyed an exceptionally detailed and well-organised three weeks in China. Unfortunately, John Chinnery became ill shortly after the party landed at Kai Tak Airport, Hong Kong. Two days later he had a heart attack in Guangzhou (then known to us as Canton). Thanks to prompt action by a medically qualified SCA delegate, Dr Mary Findlay, and first class treatment (including acupuncture) from the Chinese health service, he survived and lived for another 38 years. However, he was far too ill to lead the tour and had to stay in hospital for the duration.

Fortunately, another 'old China hand' in the SCA delegation was able to stand in for him. The Reverend John R. Fleming (1910-1999) was a divinity lecturer at St Andrews University and had been a Church of Scotland missionary in China before the People's Liberation Army victory. He hadn't been back since 1950. His life story was eventful, to say the least[7]. Like John Chinnery, John Fleming spoke fluent Mandarin, so the tourists

---

the use of the word 'Anglo' in SACU's name, a decision was taken to start a society to promote direct people-to-people links between Scotland and China.'

[6] In retrospect Chinnery may appear to have been gullible but, in his defence, back in 1956 very few people were aware of the extent of Mao's megalomania and its horrifying results. The 'Great Leap Forward' and the resulting famine that killed an estimated 35 million Chinese, had not yet begun. SACU co-founder Han Suyin, on the other hand, was certainly a fellow traveller and apologist, although not in the same class as Edgar Snow, the first western journalist to interview Mao after the Long March. Ostensibly an independent writer, in 1937 he regurgitated Mao's self-serving boasts and falsehoods in the hugely influential book *Red Star over China*. This factually inaccurate work, edited by the Chinese Communist Party's censors, was widely translated and persuaded millions of readers (including the present writer, it must be admitted) that, despite the violence of the Chinese revolution, Mao was basically a decent fellow with the interests of the peasants and the working class at heart. In 1953 the British writer Basil Davidson published *Daybreak in China*, an account of his officially sponsored tour of the country the previous year, in which he, like Snow before him, was duped by Mao and his public relations outfit. Davidson's book was almost as influential as Snow's in getting Mao a good press in the West.

[7] John Fleming's papers are preserved in the Edinburgh University Archives at New College, with an introductory biographical note as follows:

In 1938 ... [he] determined to become a missionary in Manchuria. He was married in the same year to Pearl Clark Kerr (1911-1993) whom he had known since school in Glasgow. The Flemings sailed for China in August 1938. They spent six months studying the language in Peking, then moved to Hsin Min in Manchuria. They continued their studies but also became involved in the work of the church and teaching. In the spring of 1941 they moved to Liaoyang where Fleming was responsible, in partnership with the Chinese, for co-ordinating the work of the churches in the area and where his wife taught English. However, a few months later, with the approach of war the Flemings were persuaded to leave Manchuria. They hoped to go to India and then to enter western China but were delayed for four months in Singapore. Then the ship taking them to India was bombed and sank so they also spent some time recuperating in Jakarta. Once in India they worked until the end of 1942 in Ajmer,

from Scotland were not entirely dependent on the two official interpreters assigned to the group from the China Travel Service.

John Chinnery (left) and Harry Dickinson (right) in the herbal garden of the 'barefoot doctor' dispensary, Da Li People's Commune, Guangzhou, 1st September 1972. The characters on the garden wall read: 'Chinese medicine is a great treasure trove that should be explored and enhanced'.

Among the Scottish delegation was Harry Dickinson (1924-83), a lecturer in electrical engineering at Edinburgh University. Harry was a burly, blunt-speaking, humorous man from Bury, Lancashire, very proud of his degree from the University of Manchester Institute of Science and Technology ('Yoomist', as he called it). He'd been interested for some time in what was then called 'intermediate technology', also known as 'appropriate technology', and was a member of the Intermediate Technology Development Group (ITDG). This sought to encourage the use of relatively simple and inexpensive equipment to modernise agriculture and rural industry in developing countries. Harry had a particular interest in rural electrification projects and the mechanisation of agriculture.

Rajasthan, then managed to secure a flight to Chungking, Szechwan. For nearly two years they were responsible for the Church of Scotland schools at Wanxian, then returned to Scotland for furlough at the end of 1944. After the war, in 1946 the Flemings were among the few missionaries invited back to Manchuria. Fleming taught in the Mukden [now Shenyang] Theological College and worked with the International Relief Commission while his wife taught English and gave birth to a daughter in 1949. Along with many other missionaries the Flemings left Manchuria in 1950.

As a geography postgraduate student at Edinburgh I'd met Harry at a seminar on this topic, about which he found me cheerfully ignorant. He determined to enlighten me. This was entirely in line with the postgraduate research programme he ran in collaboration with Dr David Edge, the founder of an Edinburgh University department devoted to educating science students about the arts and culture and also helping liberal arts students to understand at least the basics of science.

In the summer of 1972 Harry asked if I'd like to be his note-taker and photographer on a three-week tour of China. Of course, I said, I'd be delighted, but I didn't see how I could possibly raise the money for the air fare and the sizeable sum (sizeable, that is, to an impecunious and newly married postgraduate) required by the China Travel Service for travel, accommodation, food, interpreters and guides in the People's Republic. Harry assured me that would be no problem at all. I should first join the Scotland-China Association, then apply to the university administration for funds. I did so immediately and a very kind man called Peter McIntyre, in the University Secretary's office at Old College, pointed me in the direction of the William Dickson Travelling Scholarship. William Dickson was an Edinburgh advocate and head of the National Library of Scotland. He died in 1949, the year Mao Zedong came to power. The travelling fund was in memory of his son, killed at the Battle of Jutland in 1916. In 1972 I was the only applicant so that year's allocation was all mine.

Unfortunately for my financial plans, Caryl Robertson, a friend of my then wife, heard about this and she then also applied for a place on the trip and for the William Dickson Travelling Scholarship, so the grant had to be shared. This left me rather short of funds but somehow the balance of the money was found. Our fellow travellers included an Austrian nurse (who wore her floral *dirndl* throughout the expedition, to the great astonishment of the drably uniformed locals), some of John Chinnery's students, plus Alex Reid, Edith Wright, Elsie Collier, Muriel Murdoch, Jon Church, Howard Wagstaff, Terry Nealon and Radha Sinha, a very wise Indian professor of economics at Glasgow University. There was a great deal of discussion of the respective merits of the Indian and Chinese models of economic development, which were very different. In these discussions I tended to side with Professor Sinha.

An amusing aspect of the 26-day tour was the deference shown to me at first by some of the Chinese officials we met. They seemed to assume I was the most senior member of the tour group, partly because I was still the student Rector of Edinburgh University but perhaps also on account of my beard. It appeared that in China only extremely old and revered gentlemen comrades grew facial hair. Thus I was the first to be served at our dinner for honoured foreign guests in a dining room at Beijing's Great Hall of the People (some spread, that was!) and to be offered endless free cigarettes. Once it had been tactfully explained that I was just another bearded lefty student, I took my place in the queue while Rev. Fleming, Professor Sinha and Harry Dickinson received the respectful attention that I had been mistakenly accorded.

The SCA had requested that we travel by rail rather than air within China, in order to see as much of the countryside as possible. So our entire Chinese journey of over 3,000 miles was on trains, all but one of them drawn by coal-fired steam locomotives. We travelled 'soft seat' class (there being no first class in a people's democratic dictatorship, of course) and our meals were prepared on board. Early one morning, while stopped at a rural station in Hunan province, we heard a commotion and looked out of the window to see a live pig being manhandled on board at the rear of the kitchen car. It was slaughtered (very noisily) on board and we ate it that evening.

The trains were slow, rarely going at more than 40 miles an hour and often at 25mph, so I was able to take dozens of not-too-blurred photographs of rural life as we rumbled along (although our interpreter, Gu Shu Bao, forbade me to take pictures of bridges or trains, for reasons of 'national security'). I used the photos in slide shows when I got back and then forgot about them. They recently resurfaced in our attic and, in view of the changes in China over the past half century, they are a perhaps a cultural and historical record of some value. Considering that they were taken on Ektachrome 64ASA and 160ASA film with a cheap, manually-focussed, Soviet-made Zenit 3M single lens reflex camera – and that I mostly just left the exposure settings on a 250th of a second at f8 or f11, the image quality could have been worse.

I sold some of these snaps when I wrote up the trip for a magazine called *Business Scotland*, which paid me a handsome fee, helping to defray the expense of the 20+ rolls of colour slide film I'd exposed. My article veered towards the 'useful idiot' category when I concluded that although China was a rigid dictatorship at provincial level and above, from what we'd seen there did appear to be a surprising amount of democratic discussion at 'production team' and 'brigade' level in the rural communes[8], albeit only about how to implement Party policy handed down from above, not about what policy should be.

In his report on the study tour Harry Dickinson came to very similar conclusions. These views now seem rather indulgent. Looking back, with some embarrassment, it is a comfort that, like Harry and Professor J. K. Galbraith, who was in China at the same time as us, I was not the first nor the last visitor to gain this favourable impression from a brief and carefully shepherded tour in the middle of the Cultural Revolution. Appearances can be deceptive: there was a public relations façade, of course, but constructed far more expertly than the 'Potemkin villages' that fooled visitors to Soviet Russia a generation or two earlier. As Galbraith himself admitted in his book[9] about his trip, we 'honoured foreign guests' saw only the best, carefully selected examples of life in communes and industrial workplaces. However, that does not mean everyone we spoke to was lying. Many, if not most, of the people we met appeared genuinely committed to the principles of the commune movement. And many of those principles were admirable, whatever we think of the way they were imposed on millions of Chinese peasants.

The truth is that 51 years ago China was a ruthless one-Party dictatorship that invaded the privacy of all its subjects; there was no rule of law, no separation of the powers of the

---

[8] A production team was usually a group of households, sometimes a hamlet or small village; a brigade could comprise several adjacent villages.

[9] Galbraith, J. K. 1973. *A China Passage*. André Deutsch, London. ISBN 0 233 96473 8.

legislature, the executive and the courts; the Maoist 'thought' we heard about endlessly was cynical, simplistic cant, just like Xi Jinping's today; and Mao Zedong was the greatest mass murderer of all the 20th century's mass murderers. But he's still on the banknotes, as Xi's totalitarian rule becomes ever more pervasive, deifying the old monster[10] and using computerised mass surveillance technology (which Mao would have absolutely loved) to intimidate China's people, just as Mao did with his endless campaigns of physical and psychological terror. There is still no separation of powers.

Interestingly, for all its faults democracy remains such a powerful idea that, like Mussolini, Hitler and Stalin, even Emperor Mao felt obliged to claim democratic legitimacy for his personal despotism, as we see in the phrase 'people's *democratic* dictatorship'. Like so many of his pronouncements, this was hypocrisy. The pretence continues under the regime of Emperor Xi but democracy as we understand it in Western Europe has never existed in China. At this rate it never will.

Premier Zhou Enlai and President Richard Nixon
both supping with the devil in Beijing, February 1972.
Photo: China Daily.

---

[10] The official Chinese Communist Party verdict on Mao Zedong is that he was '70% good; 30% bad'. A more realistic assessment might be '10% good; 90% bad'. Simon Winchester's verdict in *The River at the Centre of the World* (Viking, 1997) was that Mao was 'an unmitigated disaster' in the country he ruled for 27 years.

On a slow plane to China...

Direct flights from London to China did not exist in 1972. There were rather a lot of stops along the way. So when the British Overseas Airways Corporation's flight BA914 departed Heathrow on 29th August that year the Vickers VC10 aircraft took us to Hong Kong via Rome, Damascus, Dubai and Rangoon. The reasons for this route were partly to do with colonial history and partly because although the plane

A British Overseas Airways Corporation Vickers VC-10. Photo: Wikipedia.

had the range (5,800 miles) to cover the 6,000 miles with only one refuelling stop, there was not yet enough through traffic so BOAC had to pick up passengers along the way. The VC10 was a lovely plane to fly in because the four engines were all in the tail (like the old Soviet Ilyushin 62 workhorse) and the passenger cabin was thus very quiet. Even so, we were all fairly exhausted when we landed in the steaming heat of Kai Tak airport after those five take-offs and landings. On the return trip we flew in one of BOAC's first Boeing

747 jumbos but it still made so many stops – at Bangkok, Tehran, Tel Aviv and Zurich this time – that it took over 24 hours to reach Heathrow. Some of the poor passengers had been on board even longer, since the plane left Sydney, calling at Darwin *en route* to 'Honkers'.

Not that I was complaining, even if the airport security goons in the Damascus transit lounge were rather unfriendly (although they were pussycats compared with the menacing thugs in Israeli Defence Force uniforms who boarded our plane at Tel Aviv on the way back and removed a young Japanese passenger).

This was the longest flight I'd ever made and, being a geographer, I found the views sensationally interesting. Sleep was impossible. Over India I saw enormous floods and spectacular soil erosion in the valley of the Godavari and the Eastern Ghats; there was more flooding in Burma (as it then was) and at Rangoon (ditto) the runway was surrounded by rice paddies where

Bin Dinh airbase, South Vietnam, 30th August 1972.

9

farmers and their water buffaloes worked, apparently oblivious to the roar of jet engines just 100 yards away; from 29,000 feet above Thailand I could see new roads being cut through the jungle around the Tonle Sap lake; taking coffee over Cambodia I looked down on signs of defoliation and massive destruction, thanks to the war criminal and carpet bomber Henry Kissinger, whose next job had been to arrange Nixon's visit to China.

While enjoying a lavish BOAC lunch high above the Vietnam War ('Some wine with your *boeuf bourguinon*, sir?' – and this was in steerage class) there were more signs of damage by Kissinger's notorious 'Agent Orange' defoliant sprays, bomb craters and ruined villages; and the shocking sprawl of the vast American airbase on the coast at Bin Dinh was impossible to miss. On this day, 30th August 1972, troops of the Provisional Revolutionary Government of Vietnam took two villages from the South Vietnamese Army just north of our flight path.

A bad start in Hong Kong

A shaky shot on the approach to Kai Tak Airport, Hong Kong. 30th August 1972.

My notebook shows that I was not impressed by my first sight of Hong Kong:

> *'The postcards don't show the shanty towns behind the shanty tower blocks: public AND private squalor. Most of the slums are NEW – designed as such. How does anyone stay nice in this place?'*

To be fair to Hong Kong, I was jetlagged and also had a bad cold.

To the border station

I was feeling much better on 31st August when we assembled at the pleasant, airy and almost deserted Lok Ma Chau railway station on the Hong Kong side of the border. We walked across the bridge over the river to the village of Shenzhen and boarded a diesel electric train for the journey to Guangzhou [Canton]. This was the only train we saw in China that was not hauled by a steam locomotive. We were ushered into a 'soft seat' carriage where the only other passenger was an elegant woman who may have been a Hong Kong business executive. Or perhaps she was a very senior Communist Party cadre?

The view from Lok Ma Chau station on the border of Hong Kong's New Territories and the People's Republic of China. 31st August 1972. Although the new city of Shenzhen has obliterated the once sleepy villages on the Chinese side of the river, on the Hong Kong side there are still paddy fields.

Cleaners at work in the almost deserted border Lok Ma Chau station.

Elegance in the 'soft seat' carriage of the Shenzhen to Guangzhou train.

Shenzen tower blocks and the border station at Lok Ma Chau, 2022. Google Maps.

Flagpole at the border.

A hamlet and rice paddies seen from the Shenzhen-Guangzhou train. Note the electricity poles. 31st August 1972.

A level crossing on the Shenzhen-Guangzhou line. The hand cart has a traditional timber brake but pneumatic tyres. The man hauling a heavy load of stone for the road embankment appears to be examining his hands for blisters.

Guangzhou looking north from the Temple of the Six Banyan Trees. 3rd September 1972.

Roof-scape with bamboo scaffolding, Guangzhou.

Guangzhou city sights

City view from the Temple of the Six Banyan Trees, Guangzhou.

Guangzhou was a shock after Hong Kong's traffic jams. Although there was extensive air pollution it mostly came from coal-burning factories and power stations on the outskirts. The tree-lined streets of the old colonial city were almost entirely devoid of cars and their exhaust fumes. It was a town of bicycles, hand carts and the occasional small motor tricycle van – a machine that immediately delighted Harry Dickinson as it reminded him of a 'Bradford Van'. The Chinese version had a very dirty two-stroke motorbike engine but it was a cheap, handy and practical vehicle, easily maintained in basic workshops.

After checking in at the Yang Cheng (Goat Town[11]) Hotel the political education began immediately: our hosts bussed us to the People's Park, site of

Street scene with tricycle van and acacia trees, Guangzhou. 1st September 1972.

[11] The goat is the emblem of Guangzhou.

the 1927 massacre of communists by Chiang Kai Shek. The message was clear: Mao Zedong = good; Chiang Kai Shek = bad. The nearby Museum of Archaeology reminded us how primitive things had been in imperial and prehistoric China. After lunch we visited the Institute of Peasant Studies where Mao is said to have taught 300 cadres in 1926.

Guangzhou Peoples Park Martyrs' Memorial. The slogan reads: 'Thousands and thousands of martyrs have died bravely before us for the benefit of the people; let us hold their banners high, step on their blood and march on!'

Professor Radha Sinha (left) of Glasgow University and our guide Gu Shu Bao meet a Guangzhou boy in the People's Park. 3rd September 1972.

Guangdong is mainly a flat city so for a panoramic view of downtown we climbed the pagoda at the Temple of the Six Banyan Trees. From there we saw the domestic life of the city's rooftop dwellers. They must have been flooded out that night, in a tremendous downpour accompanying the most violent thunderstorm I've ever seen. On that first

Guangzhou roof terrace.

evening in the People's Republic we watched a ferocious 'friendly' table tennis match between Sweden and China at the stadium

Temple of the Six Banyan Trees, Guangzhou.

across the road from our hotel. This too was political: we were reminded that the rapprochement between the USA and China had come about through sport, when in 1971 an American table tennis team accepted an invitation to visit, ahead of Nixon's mission. That was the public relations story. In truth secret contacts had been taking place behind the scenes some time before the much-publicised 'ping pong diplomacy'.

Traffic on the Pearl River, Guangzhou.

Pavilion of the Archaeology Museum, Guangzhou.

View from the Temple of the Six Banyan Trees, Guangzhou. 3rd September 1972.

抓革命 促生产
促工作 促战备

Poster in Guangzhou People's Park to remind the people of the Party's priorities: 'Focus on the Revolution, Promote Production, Promote Work, Promote War Preparation.'

One of the richest cities in China: the view in 2020 from the Temple of the Six Banyan Trees, Guangzhou. Part of the old city is still visible in the left-hand corner. Google Maps.

Another view from the Temple of the Six Banyan Trees, Guangzhou.

Guangzhou roof terraces and hotel.

Guangzhou carters delivering baskets of coal dust, to be made into briquettes used for domestic heating and cooking.

There was no escape from political slogans: Guangzhou street scene near the city's No. 2 Hospital.

A gigantic International Workers' Solidarity propaganda poster dwarfing pedestrians outside the Guangzhou People's Park. 3rd September 1972. It reads: 'Long live the great unity of the peoples of the world!'

Da Li Commune: 'market gardening on a continental scale'

During our tour we visited five people's communes; Da Li near Guangzhou; the Sino-Cuban Friendship commune near Beijing; Ho La commune outside Wuxi; the July First commune in the suburbs of Shanghai; and a very poor village in Dongfang People's Commune in the delta near Guangzhou which I suspect we visited by accident.

The people's communes were central to Mao Zedong's vision of China's future. With a rapidly growing population and only 11% of the country's land area suitable for crop growing, intensive agriculture and even more intensive horticulture were essential if China was to feed its people. In a famous phrase, the British writer and Mao sympathiser Basil Davidson described the view of Chinese farmland from a plane as he landed in the country for the first time in 1952: 'Market gardening on a continental scale'.

For centuries food production had been held back by feudal land tenure where most peasants in this vast patchwork of tiny fields were poor tenant farmers, forced to pay their landlords huge rents in kind (often 50% of their crop and sometimes as much as 90%). Land reform was a major factor in persuading millions of peasants to support the Chinese Communist Party. Almost the first act of the Party on taking power in 1949 was to extend nationwide the forcible (and often murderous) removal of the landowning class. This violent process had been going on for up to 20 years in communist-controlled areas. Davidson had arrived in China just as the peasants were rejoicing at getting their share of the land but he published his book[12] in 1953, a few years before Mao took the precious family plots back again in the disastrous collectivisation drive of the late 1950s[13]. Soon the State would be taking an even greater share of the crop than the landlords had done, leaving the peasants who'd grown it to starve.

At Da Li, as at every other commune, workplace or institution we visited, before seeing what was really going on we were greeted by the Revolutionary Committee and subjected to some boilerplate Maoist propaganda. The chair explained that the committee comprised representatives of the People's Liberation Army, Party cadres and experts, the militia and 'the masses'. It was not quite clear how these members were elected or selected. It was not entirely democratic, we heard, but 'there are too many things to do at

Interpreter Gu Shu Bao, Caryl Robertson and two residents of the Da Li People's Commune, Guangzhou. 1st September 1972.

---

[12] Davidson, B., 1953. *Daybreak in China*. Jonathan Cape, London.

[13] Mao argued that family-owned smallholdings were 'inefficient' (he was wrong, as so often) so he ordered that they be organised first into 'mutual aid teams' (i.e. co-operatives) and then, a few years later, into huge communes that proved unworkable and were then subdivided. All of these calamitous changes were presented as decisions by 'the masses'. The peasants never did get back their landed property but individual families and enterprises are now permitted to rent state-owned land, in addition to the small private plots that were restored to them during and after the Cultural Revolution.

present'. All the committee members were enthusiastic about the need for self-criticism and these declarations appeared to be genuine. We were told by several that it was impossible to describe to outsiders what it felt like to be part of the Maoist movement. They felt it was not just another revolution but a daring and self-conscious experiment. A bit like 17th century English Puritans with their 'City on a Hill', I thought.

Everything we saw was, of course, a huge success, due solely to the scientific application of Mao Zedong Thought in all fields of work, be it rice cultivation, carp farming, the pig farm, the electric motor assembly plant, ferro-cement sampan manufacture, rural health care or whatever. Everyone was now 'united in serving the broad masses', following 'correction of the errors' of Liu Shaoqi and his 'Capitalist Roaders'[14]. We quickly learned not to ask too many questions about Liu Shaoqi, Mao's former 'close comrade in arms' and chosen successor, who (unknown to foreigners and to most Chinese) had died of ill treatment three years previously, denied medical attention on Mao's orders and vilified by Prime Minister Zhou Enlai as 'a criminal traitor, enemy agent and scab in the service of the imperialists, modern revisionists and the Kuomintang reactionaries' – Zhou was never one to mince Mao's words[15].

Even further off limits was any discussion of the more recent death of Lin Biao, the People's Liberation Army's greatest military strategist and, until 13th September 1971, Vice-Chairman of the Chinese Communist Party – Mao's new right hand yes-man. On that day Lin Biao died when a British-made Trident aircraft carrying him and members of his family crashed in Mongolia after running out of fuel. Lin's son had commandeered the Government plane in a panic after his father fell out with Mao. The allegation, probable but never proven, was that Lin Biao planned to assassinate Mao and re-unite China under the Kuomintang. Knowing Mao's ruthlessness from their days as comrades on the Long March and before, Lin was aware that he was about to be arrested and shot after a show trial (or perhaps even without one). The story was fascinating but, like the alleged wickedness of Liu Shaoqi, Lin Biao's demise was definitely not something our hosts wished to discuss[16]. Both of the disgraced leaders have since been posthumously rehabilitated to some extent. Like Mao, both had blood on their hands from long before the Liberation.

---

14 A 'capitalist roader' was someone who thought there was merit in letting people have private plots to grow food (and maybe sell some to the State or private customers) and in allowing small businesses such as itinerant pedlars and market stallholders to operate legally.

15 Unknown to us or anyone else outside Communist Party HQ, at the time of our visit Zhou Enlai was falling out of favour with the dictator, like Liu Shaoqi and Lin Biao before him. Zhou's offence was that he was a moderating influence on Mao's ultra-left policies. Mao was also jealous of Zhou's high profile and favourable media coverage during the Nixon visit (when Mao, who'd been at death's door with pneumonia the previous month, had to be stuffed full of drugs to make him presentable and coherent for the photo opportunity). In a characteristically cruel decision, Mao would eventually cause Zhou's death in 1976, by denying him permission for an urgent cancer operation.

16 Frank Dikötter's account in *The Cultural Revolution* (Bloomsbury, 2016) is one of the best.

Prosperity built on 'night soil'

After the ritual platitudes from the Revolutionary Committee, the visit to Da Li was a fascinating delight. People seemed genuinely pleased to meet us and proudly showed us their commune's achievements, which were indeed remarkable when you consider the miseries rural Chinese peasants had endured under the old feudal landlords, then suffered during the Japanese war, the civil war and, perhaps worst of all, in the famine caused by Mao's 'Great Leap Forward' and forced collectivisation of agriculture in 1958-62. This was the worst famine in human history. It led to an estimated 35 million deaths[17]. No-one mentioned it to us when we were in China. That disaster was followed just three years later by the upheaval of Mao's Cultural Revolution, which killed another two million people and lasted from 1965 until Mao's death in September 1976. Persecutions on the basis of a victim's social origin and ideological attitude were still going on in 1972 but by the time of our trip the terror had eased back a little following the intervention of the army when Mao became alarmed by what he had unleashed. However, the nervousness was still palpable, particularly among intellectuals and those speaking foreign languages, as the behaviour of our interpreters would show.

Manure water tank and farm track, Da Li People's Commune, Guangzhou

Despite all the upheavals, Da Li appeared to be meeting its first duty to the State – of growing enough food to feed its 63,000 inhabitants while producing a surplus of foodstuffs and other local produce for taxes-in-kind to the state. In lush rice country like Guangdong that was not too difficult, given peace and political stability. The commune was growing water chestnuts, raising pigs and fertilising its soil with animal manure. Human manure was also used. Vast quantities of 'night soil' from the city of Guangzhou were less than a day's handcart-pushing away from the fields. The pervasive smell of sewage in the countryside showed that agriculture was still mostly organic.

Water chestnuts growing in a village pond, Da Li People's Commune, Guangzhou.

Later the Chinese authorities, like their counterparts in India, would boast that they

---

17 It may have been 45 million. No-one knows. There are various estimates, although no accurate one has been published by the Chinese Communist Party. The figure of 35 million is based on Yang Jisheng's courageous research for his book *Tombstone* (Cosmos Books, Hong Kong, 2008), also quoted in McGregor, R., 2010, *The Party*. Allen Lane, London. See also Becker, J., 1996, *Hungry Ghosts*. John Murray, London.

had caught up with supposedly more 'efficient' European and North American agriculture by producing and using enormous tonnages of artificial fertilisers, herbicides and pesticides. We saw no horses or draught animals on the commune. Tillage was by the water buffaloes that we saw grazing along the ridges between rice paddies, always supervised by a small girl or boy, or an old man or woman. As far as technology went, Da Li was still mostly in the middle ages. But it was clearly extremely productive.

'All comrades can eat white rice now, thanks to Chairman Mao!'

Communist Party members on the Da Li Revolutionary Committee boasted that all comrades could now eat white rice, formerly the prerogative of the exploiting classes. This had political as well as dietary significance. We were proudly shown the equipment for husking brown rice harvested from the paddies. We also saw how every household had a jar of an additive that was sprinkled on bowls of cooked white rice to counteract health problems caused by mineral and vitamin deficiencies. This powder turned out to be made from the rice husks, which of course contained the minerals, fibre and vitamins (vitamin B being the most important) that make brown rice so much more nutritious than white. Meanwhile idealistic young people in the 'degenerate' West, some of them infantile Maoists, indeed, were buying sacks of brown, unhusked rice from advertisers in the *Whole Earth Catalog*, to feed themselves in 'alternative' communes that were rather different from the Chinese variety. Inspired partly by the Da Li Commune and partly by two old self-sufficiently expert crofters whom I knew in Shetland, I would shortly join their ranks. But that is another story...

The commune's land was still owned by the State and worked collectively but at Da Li, as elsewhere in the countryside, peasants were again being allowed to grow vegetables on

small family plots, to raise pigs and poultry on their own account in their spare time, after completing their family's allotted hours for the commune, and to sell any surplus to the state. Da Li was in a traditional market gardening district and now families were able to sell vegetables to the nearby city. The bicycle was the main form of transport. Surprisingly large amounts of horticultural produce could be hung from and balanced upon a bike.

Curious onlookers, herbal pharmacy, Da Li People's Commune, Guangzhou.

The herbal pharmacy of Da Li's 'barefoot doctor'

The pharmacist (right) and staff in the herbal garden of the 'barefoot doctor' clinic, Da Li People's Commune, Guangzhou.

One of the biggest achievements of Mao's China was the near universal provision of basic rural health care. Every commune we saw had its own hospital, some more than one, as well as clinics in most villages. The success of the 'barefoot doctors' programme has been written up elsewhere and rightly praised. The basic idea was to train rural youngsters as district nurses and paramedics who could do much of the first-aid and disease-prevention work of scarce (and more expensive) fully-qualified doctors. Fifty years later, a similar policy is evident in Scotland's 'advanced nurse practitioners' who now conduct many of the initial consultations that used to be done by GPs.

At Da Li they were proud of their local health service and particularly keen to show us the use of traditional herbal cures and treatments. In the garden of a local clinic we met the pharmacist, a charming and highly intelligent man who talked enthusiastically about his medicinal plants and their uses, with not a word about politics. He did not mention Mao Zedong.

One of the most important public health policies that the all-powerful Chinese Communist Party was able to implement throughout China was insisting on better public and private hygiene. Simple measures such as insisting that middens and manure tanks were kept a safer distance from houses, providing public toilets, clean water supplies and attempting to suppress traditional habits such as spitting in public, appeared to have had considerable success.

Ashtray/litter bin, Da Li People's Commune, Guangzhou. The characters say: 'Care for public hygiene' and 'Fruit peel bin'.

China's smoking epidemic was a different matter. Nobody was doing much about it. Tobacco was cheap or even free, because people could grow it in their private plots, particularly in the provinces of Yunnan, Guizhou and Sichuan. For labouring men in particular it was a solace in their long hours of work and compulsory political meetings. In pre-revolutionary days the Christian missionaries in China had encouraged tobacco growing as it was less harmful than opium. Mao Zedong set a bad example as a chain smoker himself. And he had not been above using opium profits in his Yenan days after the Long March.

China's barefoot doctors have had a good press but recent research, based on interviews, county and provincial records and other official documents made available to writers such as Frank Dikötter during the 1990s, suggests that many of these pioneering rural paramedics were woefully ill-trained and ill-equipped, particularly in midwifery. Jung Chang, for example, has described her own inadequate efforts as a young paramedic during the Cultural Revolution. But, an apologist for the regime would say, China could not afford Western medicine for all; traditional medicine was sometimes just as effective as modern drugs; even a partly trained barefoot doctor was a lot better than what poor country folk had before, which was nothing; all that is undeniable. Today, traditional medicine is an important part of healthcare in China and techniques such as acupuncture are widely practised in the West.

In homes of their own

Decoration above front door of owner-occupied house, Da Li People's Commune, Guangzhou.

It was a considerable surprise to discover that at Da Li, as at the other communes we visited, many people owned their own homes, although not the land upon which they were built. New houses were paid for by the worker families who occupied them, with the commune providing construction materials and some labour. We asked about planning regulations. We were told there was only 'local consensus'.

Roof detail, Da Li People's Commune, Guangzhou.

There appeared to be no homeless people and there was obvious pride in the appearance of dwellings. Families had few amenities compared with European workers' homes but on several new and refurbished houses we saw beautiful wall paintings by local artists. The buildings had single brick walls and traditional tiled roofs, the bricks and tiles being made locally. Water still had to be carried from wells. Plumbing was rudimentary and electricity apparently only used for lighting and cooling fans.

The people's fuel for heating and cooking was mainly compressed blocks of coal dust, filthy but cheap. Despite this we noticed remarkable cleanliness in what amounted to well-constructed huts, about the same size as traditional Scottish but-and-ben. Pamphlets about the basic principles of hygiene were prominently displayed. Furniture was mostly plain wooden tables and chairs, with no upholstery in sight, even in the Revolutionary Committee's rooms. Bearing in mind that this was a showpiece commune it was interesting to see that most families we visited had a radio, bicycles, a sewing machine and a clock.

We heard that houses could be bought, sold and inherited. Married daughters did not share in inheritances but apparently married sons did. Clearly, women's rights had some way to go.

In some communities the proportion of owner occupancy appeared to be higher than in Scottish towns and cities (this was a decade before the Thatcher regime's decision to sell council houses to sitting tenants). There were obvious restrictions on sales and purchases of domestic properties, with price controls, stipulations on the size of house allowed and prohibitions on a family owning more than one home. I had imagined that everyone would be living in regimented barracks and forced to use communal dining halls, as indeed many were forced to do during the first years of the Communist's drive to eradicate private property during the Great Leap Forward and to some extend in the Cultural

Traditional roofing of private houses in Da Li People's Commune, Guangzhou.

Revolution, but it seemed this was already a thing of the past. If there were any communal dining halls where attendance was compulsory, we did not see them. And every family seemed to have cooking pots, presumably acquired since the era of backyard blast furnaces – when the peasants' pots, pans and even their bedsteads and doorknobs had been melted down in the industrialisation frenzy of Mao's 'great leap backwards' in 1958-62.

Wall decoration, private house, Da Li People's Commune, Guangzhou.

A back alley with privately owned pigs, Da Li People's Commune, Guangzhou.

Eradicating illiteracy.

Kindergarten staffer and children, Da Li People's Commune, Guangzhou.

Education was another area where Communist China's progress was enormous and undeniable. Every commune we visited had nurseries and primary schools in its villages, something to which only a tiny minority had access in pre-revolutionary times. Although China was still an overwhelmingly agrarian country in 1972 (with about 80% of the population living outside cities and towns) literacy rates had improved dramatically. In 1949 it was estimated that about 90% of the rural people and 70% of urban dwellers were unable to read or write.[18] By 1972 literacy rates were over 50% in the country and 80% in the towns and cities.

What the newly literate were allowed to read was less admirable. The Communist Party's nationwide organisation reached all the way down to village, hamlet and household level. Rigorous control of access to information and the suppression of all opposition to the rigid Party line (whatever it might be at the moment) was clearly the purpose of this extraordinary system. To us westerners it seemed extremely oppressive but most Chinese seemed to accept it, given the chaos and misery that had been the lot of their parents and grandparents before 1949. There had also been a fair amount of chaos and misery in the Maoist decade before our visit. The 'Great Leap Forward' of 1958-62 had seen grain production collapse as labour and resources were diverted to a wildly unrealistic attempt to industrialise the entire country in just a few years. Much of Mao's famine was caused by farm labour shortages because peasants who should have been working in the fields were instead producing a great deal of useless, brittle pig iron in the thousands of primitive blast furnaces set up in communes, operated by people who had little knowledge of or expertise in steel making.

---

[18] See: Hamm, H. 'Revolutionary China in Transition' in Schulthess, E. (1966) *China*. Collins, London and Artemis Verlags, Zurich.

Forests were destroyed to make charcoal, air pollution was rampant and wildlife severely damaged in indiscriminate campaigns to kill small birds described by the Communist Party as 'pests' although some species targeted were also natural pest controllers of aphids and other bugs and slugs. So Mao's Great Leap was an environmental as well as a human tragedy. But it was too recent a memory for any frank public discussion, least of all with foreigners present. When I asked if there was any constructive criticism of Mao's thought the interpreters told me it would be pointless as he was infallible. They did not translate my questions.

The country was only just recovering from this Mao-made catastrophe when he started the Cultural Revolution, terrorising teachers, engineers, scientists, intellectuals and anyone else his Red Guards judged to have got above themselves and to be failing to 'serve the broad masses'. There were many opportunities for petty score settling and oppression, often leading to the torture and death of victims whose only crime might have been to be clever or enterprising, or just plain unpopular. The parallels with 17th century Scottish witch hunts were disturbing.

The Cultural Revolution would not finally end until after Mao's death in 1976, when the blame for all the trouble was put on his widow, Jiang Qing, who was certainly a vicious, paranoid, conspiratorial maniac[19] but also a convenient scapegoat. Many of the people we met in China had been scarred personally by these serial convulsions but by the autumn of 1972 things were generally more relaxed than at the height of mass hysteria a few years earlier.

After squeezing the agricultural sector for decades, with forced quotas of communal produce delivered to the State at low prices, the communes were now, in 1972, paid more for their goods. Even Mao had finally understood that you cannot eradicate rural poverty if you deliberately keep people poor. His peasant forebears in Hunan province could have told him that, of course. So the relaxed, optimistic and even happy atmosphere we detected on the showplace communes and in other workplaces was genuine, I think, even if detailed, honest examination of Mao's policies, and indeed of China's history, was still taboo.

But if this was socialism, how come some workers were paid piece rates, some paid by the hour and there were still startling pay differentials between senior cadres following the Party line and lowly minions doing menial work? Yes, the Revolutionary Committee chair told us, the wage differentials could be quite high but the distribution of income was 'very equal' i.e. 'most people get about the average'. But the 'distribution of resources' was 'remarkably equal', for example in access to hospitals, doctors, schools, teachers, housing, transport, heating, lighting, food at work, crèches, nurseries and kindergartens, pensions, etc.: 'Without doubt this is the fairest system of distribution that exists or has ever existed, in any country'.

---

[19] I do not exaggerate, as is clear from the accounts of her character and behaviour in *The Private Life of Chairman Mao* by his doctor, Zhisui Li (Arrow Books, 1996).

In most countries one would be disturbed to find four-year-old children singing songs of praise about the political leader of the present regime but, the chair insisted, 'In China it is different – the Chinese people really do have something to celebrate.'

Nursery and kindergarten children welcome the foreign visitors, Da Li People's Commune, Guangzhou.

Postcard showing Chinese Communist Party cadre addressing a mass meeting at harvest time.

Grandmother and grandchildren, Da Li People's Commune, Guangzhou.

Children saying goodbye to Jon Church, one of the foreign visitors, Da Li People's Commune, Guangzhou. 1st September 1972.

Surgeons of No. 2 Hospital, Guangzhou. 2nd September 1972. The surgeon wearing the red badge was a senior member of the Revolutionary Committee which some years earlier, during the Cultural Revolution, had taken over the management of the hospital. His more junior colleagues appeared in awe of him, as well they might be, for the Revolutionary Committee had the power to send them to the countryside for 're-education' and hard labour if judged not to be 'serving the broad masses'.

Acupuncture anaesthesia

Our delegation leader, John Chinnery, was now under intensive care in Guangzhou after his heart attack, so he was not able to accompany us on a visit to the city's No. 2 Hospital on the second day of our visit. Here, as in the Da Li herbal pharmacy, doctors were using traditional medicines as well as more modern treatments.

No. 2 Hospital was a busy place, with 780 staff looking after 550 beds and 2,500 outpatients as well as teaching medical students from Dongshan Medical College and doing scientific research. Staff also organised mobile medical teams that visited the countryside and factories to 'give priority to treatment of the broad masses'.

The most astonishing thing, for Western visitors, was to be invited to join medical students in the observation gallery above a fifth floor operating theatre, where we watched two surgical operations, both apparently carried out using acupuncture as the anaesthetic. We spoke to the patients beforehand and they confirmed that only acupuncture was being used, and that it was highly effective, as the pictures appear to confirm. Both the woman undergoing the removal of an ovarian cyst and the man having an operation to remove a stone from his ureter were conscious throughout. Neither showed the slightest sign of pain.

The surgeon explained that acupuncture was 'simpler, efficient, economical and safe'. There were 'imperfections', however: analgesia was not complete; the patient could feel tensed muscles, but there was a 90% success rate.

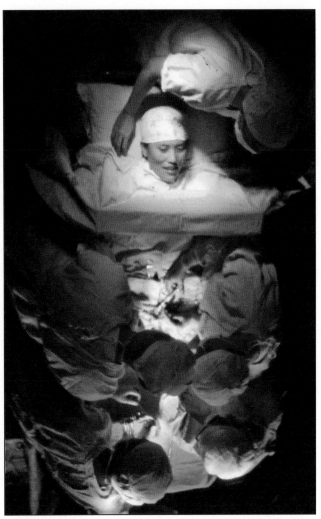

Patient under acupuncture anaesthesia during operation to remove ovarian cyst at No.2 Hospital, Guangzhou.

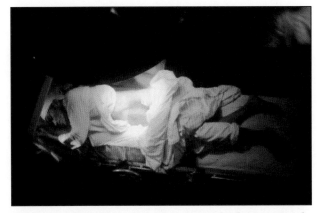

Patient undergoing urinary tract calculus removal under acupuncture anaesthesia, No.2 Hospital, Guangzhou.

He added that the simple apparatus (needles) avoided harmful after-effects of drugs. They also used acupuncture to alleviate the effects of polio and 'to treat deaf mutes'.

At a lengthy meeting with the Revolutionary Committee of Dongshan Medical College we learned that No. 2 Hospital was one of four hospitals it served. Six hundred medical students a year were being admitted, plus 200 nursing students and 150 postgraduates after their first clinical practice. There were equal numbers of male and female students.

Clearly the college had been in a fairly recent upheaval, as had all Chinese academic institutions. The Revolutionary Committee, the chair said, was founded as recently as 1969 and followed the 'three-in-one principle': 1 revolutionary cadres (i.e. (Party officials); 2 the army; and 3 'the masses of all ages'. Of the 35 Revolutionary Committee members four were students, 12 'revolutionary cadres', six from the People's Liberation Army and just 13 doctors, nurses and technicians but the proportion of doctors was not fixed because 'students who become doctors remain as student representatives'. Although the students' main job was to study (they had 'no time for administration') they were in fact making many suggestions about course content and how the college was organised.

'Students have two roles: study and revolution,' we were told: 'They take part in administration and incorporate themselves into the leadership of the colleges... help decide the teaching programme [and] discuss draft teaching plans. Students here put forward 52 proposals. We found the mass line. Discussions are prolonged. The teaching programme is in accordance with proletarian aims. Teachers and students [jointly] prepare teaching materials. All are free to comment on study and teaching. There is a new relationship between students and teachers since the Cultural Revolution.'

This, if true and not pure cant, certainly sounded like an improvement on the stuffy traditionalism associated with the administration of Edinburgh University's medical faculty in years gone by.

Before the Cultural Revolution a medical student at Dongshan had to take 36 different courses in order to qualify but investigation had shown that 'some were not immediately necessary', for example higher mathematics, and were 'eliminated for the time being'. Some courses were merged and 'repetitious' courses 'simplified'. Only 15 courses were now required. As a result, medical students could get their basic qualification after three years, whereas previously it was six.

The Revolutionary Committee was particularly proud of the 'integration of theory with practice' in teaching methods: 'The first year in the old system had no relevance to medicine and students saw no patients in their first three years of study'. That sounded familiar from what I'd heard from medical student friends in Edinburgh at that time. Now the Dongshan students learned to do common operations in their first two years and they 'did better than some of those who completed five years' study'. What the patients thought of this innovation we did not ask. Nor, presumably, had the patients.

The emphasis was on rural areas: 'Students are sent to local health centres where they spend a third of their time... Results are better, quicker and more economical.'

So it seemed the State was getting more doctors for its money, and sooner, even if they were perhaps less well qualified than before. But, as we had seen at the Da Li Commune's local clinic, this looked like a sensible approach to China's health problems, whether you were a Marxist or not.

Marxist medical education

Medical politics: Mao statue outside Dong Shan Medical College, Guangzhou.

The college might have got rid of some unnecessary courses in the syllabus but some of this padding had been replaced with (equally tedious) courses in Marxism. It wasn't all theory: in line with Mao's policy of self-reliance (self-reliance for everyone but him, that is) students helped to grow their own food and their families at home also sent them rice. 'A positive attitude to physical labour' was expected while 'studying for the revolution'. During vacations students had to report back on their studies to their home town committees who had sent them to Dongshan.

Before the Cultural Revolution the medical college had been 'divorced from proletarian politics and practice'. Now students did agricultural and industrial work and 'criticised the bourgeoisie'.

Children from 'bourgeois' backgrounds and 'non-labouring families' could still become medical students but 'local leadership and also the masses' had to approve their applications. The criteria for admission to the college had radically changed. Before the

36

Cultural Revolution all that counted was high marks. To someone from Edinburgh University that sounded reasonable but we were told that it 'ignored the kind of person and their origin'. Only high school students were eligible in the bad old days. There were no students 'from the workers and peasants with practical experience'. These people were effectively banned.

Candidates were now selected from 'workers and peasants'. The number of new student places was decided by the State plan, with quotas of places assigned to local areas. Applicants were issued with 'educational propaganda to ensure correct attitudes'.

As all education was paid for by the state, including tuition fees and a 21 yuan a month maintenance grant, ultimately the State said who could go to college and who could not. The 1972 requirements for admission were as follows:

1. Ideology – serve the people. Study the works of Marx, Engels, Stalin and Mao Zedong.
2. Practical experience of at least two years at work.
3. A cultural level equivalent to junior middle school graduates and above.
4. Age about 20, physically healthy and unmarried.

These last two flagrantly discriminatory stipulations would certainly not have been acceptable in the West. But when we came to discuss how students' progress was measured we found that China had not departed all that far from Scottish practice. Examinations were the only assessment method before the Cultural Revolution and they were still taking place. One cadre mentioned Mao's famous quotation about teachers 'attacking' students with 'surprise tactics' in exams. When we asked what other assessment methods were used to decide whether a junior doctor was competent or not, the only answer was: 'It is a changing situation'.

On graduation a junior doctor could earn a probationary salary of 51.5 yuan a month, rising to 60 or 70 yuan, much the same as a docker. This compared with 381 yuan a month for the college's highest-paid professor. No-one was going to get rich as a doctor in Red China.

There was, officially, no private medical practice in China[20]. The newly qualified doctors from Dongshan Medical College had little choice in where they would work. On graduation students were assigned to jobs 'according to the State plan and local needs'.

The State planned everything, interfering in people's private lives and career choices to an extent we pampered bourgeois Edinburgh students would have found outrageous. But our Chinese contemporaries seemed to think it perfectly reasonable. They accepted compulsory direction of labour without (audible) complaint.

We would hear more from university students and staff when we reached Beijing and Shanghai.

---

[20] Recent studies suggest that during the chaos of the Cultural Revolution there was a black market in everything, including medical advice and treatment.

Slow trains through China

Train travel was the perfect way to see China at a leisurely pace. Unlike Kissinger, Nixon and Professor Galbraith, who were whisked around by plane, we were able to observe the life of 'the broad masses' at close range. It was obvious that the Party had found something for everyone to do. We saw many roadworks and railway track improvement projects, all of them spectacularly over-staffed by Western standards. Pensioners, women, students and the larger children were all doing their bit to shift sand, gravel and rocks. It was harvest time so we also had a clear view of the work going on in the fields and farmyards as we trundled along.

It all looked very normal but a decade earlier, during Mao's great famine, there would have been starved corpses lying unburied in hovels within sight of the railway lines because their food had been stolen by the Chinese Communist Party and its local sycophants. The world outside as yet knew nothing of that nationwide catastrophe, which had been particularly severe in the provinces of Hunan and Hebei that lay

Freight train guard at Guangzhou Station, 3rd September 1972.

on our 800-mile route from Guangzhou to Zhengzhou. To us pampered tourists these provinces now appeared well-ordered, busy and even prosperous, like a scene from a bucolic Breughel harvest painting, despite obvious drought in some areas. The Chinese peasantry had survived yet another calamity, albeit probably the biggest ever visited upon them over so many suffering centuries. But, as we now know, in Hunan and Hubei many were still starving at the time of our trip, out of sight of the railways we travelled on.

No sooner was the great famine over than the Cultural Revolution broke over the peasants' heads, with more arrests of hundreds of thousands of innocent people. The railways took the victims from their home villages to prisons and camps. Stations were convenient holding pens. We noticed that most of the station buildings in small towns still had bars at the ground floor windows. These were separate from the shutters to control ventilation, their purpose being to control the freedom of movement of 'anti-Party elements', 'right opportunists' and 'counter-revolutionaries' awaiting transport to their wretched fates.

Unknown to us (or to anyone else outside China at that time), some regions had very recently been in a state of civil war, with armed clashes between rival groups of red guards and between them and the People's Liberation Army troops sent to quell the fighting. Most of the country had been under martial law and Mao's military dictatorship until the month before our delegation crossed from Hong Kong.

None of this was mentioned by our minders. Nor did we hear the truth about Mao's massive forced migration from the cities to the countryside. During the Cultural Revolution some 17 million students were rusticated and sent to remote villages to 'learn from the masses'. Those from 'bad class backgrounds' often ended up in forced labour camps where they were worked 12 hours a day, seven days a week, under military control. Many never recovered their permit to live in the towns and cities. Hundreds of thousands of families were broken up.

Leaving Guangdong at the start of our 3,000 mile train ride to Beijing and back.

A rural station in Hunan Province. Note the bars on the windows.

Farm tracks and power lines seen from the train, Hunan province.

Drought-affected village seen from the train, Hunan province. 4th September 1972.

People's Liberation Army man catching his train at a station in Hunan province.

Railway maintenance workers taking a break on the Guangzhou to Zhengzhou line.

Handcart squad shifting railway track ballast, Hunan province.

A woman carrying a traditional, home-made shoulder basket, Hubei province.

Straw ricks in the farmyard of a Hunan village.

A derelict-looking factory, possibly an artificial fertiliser plant from the Great Leap Forward.

The 'Dragon Spine Water Mover'

One of our main interests in China was seeing how 'intermediate' or 'appropriate' technology was being used to transform agriculture. Rice cultivation obviously depends on very precise control of water levels in paddy fields but further north the cultivation of wheat, millet and other cereals also requires irrigation systems, particularly in areas subject to alternating drought and floods.

At the Da Li commune workshop we had seen our first hand-cranked irrigation pump, known as the 'dragon spine water mover'. Sometimes these pumps were operated by foot pedals, which was more efficient (the leg muscles usually being stronger).

It was a surprisingly efficient machine but required an enormous amount of labour. Shortage of labour was not a problem but

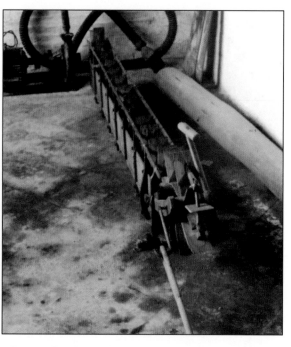

The mechanism of a hand-powered 'dragon spine water mover', sitting on the workshop floor next to a small electric pump in the Da Li People's Commune, Guangzhou. 1st September 1972.

Two hand cranked dragon-spine-water-movers in use to irrigate rice paddies, seen from the Guangzhou-Zhengzhou train passing through Hunan province. Each machine had two crews, one doing the exhausting work and the other taking a much-needed break. In the background are new electricity poles.

43

feeding China's growing population was, so anything that could improve the efficiency of irrigation was a priority.

The original dragon spine water movers were hand-made out of wooden components. The model we saw had some metal parts, including a steel frame, but was still basically the same ingenious, home-made machine that had been used for centuries.

Harry Dickinson was delighted: this was the 'appropriate' technology we had come to see. But it was also 'intermediate' technology because big changes were on the way and this ingenious pump would soon be obsolete. Substituting electric pumps for dragon spine water movers was one of the first things the communes in south China went for as the electricity grid was extended to villages, farmsteads and, as we saw throughout the countryside of Guangdong, Hunan and Hubei provinces, the power lines were taken right out into the fields wherever possible.

It's important to bear in mind that our trip only took us through the more prosperous parts of lowland China. What was happening in remoter, more mountainous districts further west we could not tell, but it was certainly made clear to us wherever we went that electrification was seen by the Party and the people as the biggest single boost to rural productivity. That the electricity used was at that time largely generated by burning coal did not seem to be a concern. This was long before some of the very large hydro-electricity projects such as the Three Gorges Dam on the Yangtze Kiang.

The dragon spine water mover's replacement (1): a pump house for an electrically powered irrigation system near Hangzhou.

The dragon spine water mover's replacement (2): a diesel-powered irrigation pump mounted on a ferro-cement 'dragon boat' sampan at Ho La People's Commune, Wuxi.

Electricity poles in village fields, Hunan province.

A new irrigation pumping station nearing completion on the south bank of the Huang He (Yellow River) near Zhengzhou. 6th September 1972. Note the tree planting under way on the newly constructed terraces. This project was not far from a massive canal, built by hand in the 1950s, which had proved completely useless.

Harry Dickinson pausing for a breather at the Zhengzhou irrigation station. He was already suffering from the heart problems that would kill him 11 years later, at the age of only 58.

Soil erosion in the hills near Zhengzhou. 6th September 1972.

One of the sluices on the Zhengzhou irrigation project.

Look! There are foreigners in the new pagoda'

A crowd gathered in Zhengzhou town centre to see the foreigners who had climbed to the top of the famous double pagoda. 5th September 1972.

It was clear on our arrival at Zhengzhou that foreigners were a rare sight in the city. Hundreds of people stopped to stare as our China Travel Service guides escorted us to the top of a remarkable new, twin-towered pagoda at a major intersection, from which we had a good view of the city, and the citizens of us. The two minibuses laid on for us also attracted attention from oxcart drivers and from construction workers busy repairing roads, footpaths and bridges. There was no shortage of work to do and plenty of people to do it. In the West it would be called overmanning; here it was called full employment but it was obvious that the workers still had plenty of time for tea and smoke breaks.

Zhengzhou townscape in the rain.

Zhengzhou rooftops in September 1972. Below is a view from the same pagoda in 2022.

In this 2022 Google Maps view the twin pagoda is almost the only surviving building from 50 years ago at the junction of Minggong Road and Jiefang Road.

49

Zhengzhou town centre after 30 years of 'Socialism with Chinese characteristics': a 2022 Google Street View of the pagoda, now surrounded by commercial brutaliths and advertisement hoardings. It is not an ancient pagoda, having been built in 1971 to commemorate the 1927 strike by railway workers and others at this strategic road, rail and river junction.

A timber yard viewed from the pagoda in Zhengzhou town centre. 5th September 1972.

Breaking our interpreter Gu Shu Bao's injunction not to photograph bridges, I snapped this construction crew of nine men rebuilding a rail bridge in Zhengzhou, when our minibus gave way to an ox cart driver. 6th September 1972.

Roadside tea break for a Party of women workers in Zhengzhou.

Art serving the people

Mao had often said that all art, music and literature was for the masses and here in the middle of China in the middle of the Cultural Revolution, our hosts were keen that we experienced some ideologically sound entertainment. So, on our first evening in Zhengzhou, we were taken to see a revolutionary opera, *The Red Lantern*. The plot was simple (Mao Zedong good; Kuomintang bad), the dancing spectacular, the singing spirited and the simple tunes superficially attractive but soon becoming repetitive.

A scene from a more recent production of The Red Lantern. Photo: China Daily/Wikipedia.

After the show I bought two LPs from our hotel's gift shop. Some track titles from '*Chairman Mao, You Are The Red Sun In Our Hearts*' give a flavour of the diversity and originality of Chinese musical culture during the Cultural Revolution:

1. 'Sing in Praise of the Great, Glorious and Correct Communist Party of China'
2. 'Red Guards from the Grasslands see Chairman Mao'
3. 'We Wish Chairman Mao a Long, Long Life!'

The album '*Five Revolutionary Songs of The Shensi-Kansu-Ningsia Border Region*' was a little more varied, but not much:

1. 'Our Leader Mao Tse Tong'
2. 'Red Lilies Crimson and Bright'
3. 'The Armymen and People Join in the Production Drive'
4. 'Workers and Peasants have Taken up Arms'
5. 'Joy of Emancipation'

One of my musical souvenirs of the Cultural Revolution.

According to the sleeve notes, 'these revolutionary folk songs came into being and prevailed' in the Shensi-Kansu-Ningsia Border region at the time after 1935 when Mao had his headquarters there, at Yenan, the capital[21]. As for the 'joy of emancipation', later accounts suggest that most of the population of Yenan was very glad to see the back of Mao when he and his gangsters moved on to terrorise and extort food from peasants elsewhere.

---

[21] I still have these lamentable recordings. Out of pure mischief, I once played the instrumental version of 'Our Leader Mao Tse Tong' *[sic]* on BBC Radio Shetland, to see if my BBC bosses would notice. They didn't, but I noticed that The Rolling Stones' track 'Dead Flowers' *was* on the corporation's list of banned songs, along with a Janis Joplin number and much of Tom Waits' output, all of about the same vintage as the Cultural Revolution.

Jade carving and a 'bumper crop'

We all had a good time in Zhengzhou and wished we could have stayed longer. Harry Dickinson reckoned it was the best part of the trip. He got on famously with the expert carvers at an arts-and-crafts factory producing jade works for export and domestic markets; at the Zhengzhou Fruit Orchard Farm he made friends with an apple breeder, whom he dubbed 'the Chinese Walter Gabriel'.[22] We inspected this elderly comrade's 'bumper crop' of apples in field trials of varieties developed in the laboratories of the Zhengzhou Fruit Research Centre.

At the obligatory meeting with the Revolutionary Committee we discussed problems with chemical pesticides and the benefits of biological controls. Mao's Thought was helping them a lot, of course. Harry had little time for the bureaucrats. He dedicated his report on our researches in China to the 'pragmatic' working folk he met in Zhengzhou. They reminded him of his origins in Lancashire.

A skilled worker at the Zhengzhou jade figurine factory. 5th September 1972.

Zhengzhou jade factory workers telling Harry Dickinson about their pay and conditions.

Our China Travel Service interpreter, Gu Shu Bao, proudly displaying the 'bumper crop' apple variety bred at the fruit research centre outside Zhengzhou.

---

[22] After the rustic sage character in the BBC radio serial 'The Archers'.

No. 3 Cotton Mill, Zhengzhou.

Cotton mills are notoriously bad for their workers' health: of necessity, they are usually very hot and damp; and the air is always full of tiny fibres that can cause respiratory infections and lung damage.

Zhengzhou's No. 3 Textile Factory was no exception but as far as we could see the conditions here were no worse than average and probably better than in some other Asian countries' mills.

The mill made some artificial fibres as well as spinning cotton and weaving textiles. Many, though not all, of the workers were wearing

Dangerous, hot and humid working conditions in the Zhengzhou cotton mill.

The factory floor of No. 3 Cotton Mill, Zhengzhou.

face masks but some of the machinery was unguarded. Under Mao, workers who sustained an industrial or agricultural injury were honoured as having made a glorious sacrifice for socialism.

As in most of the Chinese workplaces we visited, childcare was provided. We enjoyed a delightful concert put on by the factory's kindergarten.

A machine minder masked up against airborne lint particles, No. 3 Cotton Mill, Zhengzhou. 5th September 1972.

This show was much more fun than the routine interview with the Revolutionary Committee, where it was clear that we were in the presence of a petty tyranny, dressed up as workers' control. As had happened everywhere else under the 'proletarian' dictatorship, the trade unions had been subsumed into the management. No independent labour organisation was possible, far less any thought of strikes.

This was the closest we got to Mao Zedong: Tianan Men, Beijing. 10th September 1972.

The 'broad masses' exploring the Forbidden City.

My Summer Palace camouflage

The tour wasn't entirely taken up by studies of rural development technology and lengthy meetings with earnest Revolutionary Committee cadres; in Beijing, where we arrived on an overnight sleeper train from Zhengzhou, we 'did the sights' for a couple of days.

My pictures are like those everyone takes there. The only unusual thing about the snaps is that in 1972 there were almost no other foreign tourists.

The author's less than successful attempt to look like a local at the Emperors' Summer Palace, Beijing. The Mao jacket was a hard-wearing garment and served me well in later years when I was working on a croft co-operative in Shetland (an enterprise known to our local neighbours, inaccurately, as the 'commune').

In the Forbidden City, almost the only foreign visitors were the Scotland-China Association delegates and the cabin crew of a Japanese airliner.

A father, son and grandson on a day trip from the countryside marvel at a huge bronze urn in the Palace courtyard, Beijing. 10th September 1972.

This amused Chinese sightseer had just noticed the 'foreign devil' wearing a Mao jacket. Palace Museum, Beijing.

This group of Chinese sightseers, however, seemed less amused at having a 'foreign devil' taking their photograph without asking. Summer Palace, Beijing.

The renovated Temple of Heavenly Peace, Beijing.

Worker and peasant families enjoying a sunny Saturday afternoon in the gardens of the Summer Palace, Beijing, with a People's Liberation Army man posing in the background. Note the blue sky and unpolluted air.

The fabric of the Forbidden City and other historic buildings in Beijing had been deliberately neglected during the Cultural Revolution. To spruce the place up for foreign tourists bearing pounds, dollars and yen, this man was clearing weeds from between the cobblestones of the Palace Museum courtyard.

Meeting the expatriates

In Beijing we met some British expatriates who'd stayed on after 1949 and others who'd settled there after the Communist Party dictatorship was established. They presumably thought the sacrifice of 70 million[23] Chinese lives had been worth it in the ongoing struggle to achieve communism. They were the victims of propaganda, of course, but also of self-delusion, 'useful idiots', as Leon Trotsky had called such people in revolutionary Russia. They were certainly useful to the Great, Glorious and Correct Chinese Communist Party and its Helmsman, the Red Sun in their Hearts. But if these Western scholars and journalists had not lived and worked in China during the 1950s, 60s and 70s, the rest of us would have known even less about what was going on there. They kept the door ajar, if not fully open.

We met a few of them, not by chance but because our hosts thought we should meet them. Later, in Shanghai (see below, p.123), we interviewed Carl and Paul Crook, two of the three sons of David and Isabel Crook, the Marxist couple who in 1959 had co-authored an influential and sympathetic account of Mao's rural policies[24]. When the Cultural Revolution began they were among the 300-400 Westerners who lived most of the time in the capital, comfortably employed in state-financed organisations such as the Foreign Languages Institute, where sympathetic expatriates wrote and translated Maoist propaganda[25].

David, Isabel and Carl Crook, 1952. Photo: BBC/Crook Family Archive.

Isabel Crook, born in China to Canadian missionary parents, was an anthropologist by training and later a much admired university lecturer who taught English to many of China's future diplomats and ambassadors. In the early days of the Cultural Revolution she and her husband made the mistake of taking a family holiday in the UK (their first since 1947). This, as well as David's wartime service with the RAF, aroused the suspicions of Mao's ignorant and infantile Red Guard zealots, even though during

---

[23] Estimates vary of the number of people who died as a result of Mao Zedong's policies and actions between 1922 and 1976, but most sources agree it was at least 70 million.

[24] Crook, D. & I. 1959. *Revolution in a Chinese Village: Ten Mile Inn*. Routledge edition 1979. ISBN 9780710033932. The book described in detail the life of peasants in pre-revolutionary China and the changes wrought by revolution in one village.

[25] For an insight into the role of these tame writers, see Chapter 20 of Becker, J. 1996. *Hungry Ghosts – China's Secret Famine*, John Murray, London. ISBN

his vacation David had done a lecture tour in the USA, trying to explain and justify the Cultural Revolution to bemused American audiences.

On 17th October 1967 a group of Red Guards seized David and took him to a Beijing prison[26] where he was charged with being a British spy[27] and later convicted. They placed Isabel under house arrest soon afterwards and she was detained *incommunicado* on the university campus for three years. Her young sons had no idea where she was.

In January 1973 David Crook was at last released, two years after Isabel's detention ended. Not long afterwards they were exonerated at a grand reception where Prime Minister Zhou Enlai, just risen from his hospital bed, apologised in person to them and other Cultural Revolution victims. He did so in front of an embarrassed and disapproving Madame Mao, Jiang Qing, whose followers had been responsible for their sufferings. As compensation, the Crooks were given well-paid jobs and pensions for life. David spent his later years helping to produce a Chinese-English dictionary.

Disgusted and disillusioned, Carl, Paul and their brother Michael left China a few months afterwards, astonished that despite all he had suffered their 'ultra-leftist' father remained loyal to Mao, his argument being that on the 'long march' from feudalism to communism there were bound to be 'mistakes and wrong turnings'. David Crook died in Beijing in 2000, aged 90. Isabel, at the time of writing (January 2023), is still living there, at the age of 107. She explained why in a 2020 film in which she appeared with Paul: 'We belonged and that is why we stayed.'[28] Paul, who did not stay, went on to a distinguished 30-year career with the BBC World Service's China section.

David and Isabel Crook were sincere believers and by no means the worst of the regime's apologists, who included writers such as Anna Louise Strong, an elderly American communist bigot who denied the existence of the 1958-62 famine[29]. Strong should have known better, as she had been in the USSR at the time of the Ukraine famine in the 1930s which, like Mao's copycat crimes, was caused by forced collectivisation, almighty lies and punitive State grain requisitions.

---

[26] See: Crook, D., 1991. The Ballad of Beijing Jail. http://www.davidcrook.net/pdf/DC15_Chapter12.pdf

[27] He was not but, as a committed Stalinist in the 1930s, he did spy for the USSR in Shanghai and in Spain during the Civil War.

[28] This beguiling China Global Television Network (CGTN) film about Isabel is online at: https://www.youtube.com/watch?v=1Lyoq4MSTd8. Funded by the Chinese Government, the film of course makes no mention of the Cultural Revolution. It also perpetuates some fictions about the Long March, fictions which have become factoids in the CCP's rigorously policed version of the history of the People's Republic of China. For example: the famous chain suspension bridge that the People's Liberation Army is supposed to have crossed under a hail of Kuomintang bullets had not in fact lost all of its timber slats, just a few of them, and there were no Kuomintang units in the area at the time, so the People's Liberation Army crossed it unopposed (Mao being carried on a litter, as usual); see Jung, C. and Halliday, J. 2005, *op. cit.*

[29] See her mendacious book of Maoist propaganda: Strong, A. L., 1959. *The Rise of the Chinese People's Communes – and Six Years After*. New World Press [Chinese Communist Party], Beijing.

The redoubtable Rose Smith

On our last day in Beijing we had lunch with a founding member of the Communist Party of Great Britain (CPGB). Rose Smith, then aged 81, was a remarkable character. Born in Putney, London, in 1891, she became a pioneering women's trade union organiser during the First World War when she worked in munitions factories in the mining town of Mansfield, Nottinghamshire.

A trained teacher, she found herself debarred from her profession when she got married in 1916. She joined the CPGB in 1922 and there the sexist discrimination continued: because she was married and had three-year-old twin sons, the Party put her on a 'probationary list'. Despite this, Rose became a full-time organiser for the Party in 1929, the year after women over 21 gained the same voting rights as men in British elections. She was twice unsuccessful as a CPGB general election candidate, on the second attempt being imprisoned for three months because she'd joined a picket line during a strike. In 1932 she moved to Bolton, Lancashire, where she led the Women's Hunger March and was elected to the CPGB's central committee. She was a journalist on the communist newspaper *Daily Worker* from 1942 to 1955 and then retired – but immediately became active in the Campaign for Nuclear Disarmament.

That would have been enough excitement for most people but in 1962, at the age of 71, after a brief sojourn with one of her sons who'd settled in Australia, Rose Smith moved to Beijing and took a job with the Foreign Languages Press. A conversation with Zhou Enlai during the Sino-Soviet split of 1960 had persuaded her to follow Mao's line. The CPGB backed the USSR so, as a result, Rose lost touch with many old comrades in the UK. Later she wrote propaganda for the Xinhua News Agency. During the Cultural Revolution Rose left China and for a while worked at a nursing home in Chesterfield, Derbyshire. Why she left and why she'd returned to Beijing by 1972, we were not told. Her life story[30] was extraordinary but, alas, her views on the current state of Chinese politics appeared to follow faithfully the Chinese Communist Party's official line. To be fair, the Party probably kept her as ignorant of the truth as it did us. We had a second encounter with Rose in Shanghai but again she spilled no beans although, as a confidante of senior cadres, she must have known much more than she said. She appeared to have no regrets.

---

[30] Rose Smith died in Beijing in 1985 at the age of 94. See: Fong, G. C. M. (1998) *The times and life of Rose Smith in Britain and China, 1891-1985: an interplay between community, class and gender.* Ph.D. thesis, Concordia University, Montreal, Canada. https://spectrum.library.concordia.ca/id/eprint/469/

See also her profiles on Wikipedia and in *Socialist Worker*, 4th June 2005: https://socialistworker.co.uk/features/rose-smith-a-woman-communist-at-the-heart-of-the-struggle/

A visit to the Sino-Cuban Friendship Commune

Four generations of the same family at the Sino-Cuban Friendship Commune near Beijing. Note our 'housewife' interviewee's watch, a sign of relative affluence and perhaps political influence.

The filling in our Beijing tourism sandwich was a very interesting visit to the Sino-Cuban Friendship Commune just outside the city limits.

Here we had another chance to see the rural (or, at least, suburban) health care system. We interviewed a village 'barefoot doctor' who had started his initial six months of training in 1966, the year the Cultural Revolution disrupted schools, colleges and universities. After that he had 'practical training'. Now he covered his district by bicycle. He reminded us that before 1949 there had been 'only one bike' in his village.

In China the People's Liberation Army are never far away. Fifty years ago they were almost the only people with access to modern motor vehicles. This People's Liberation Army jeep was available to transport patients to hospital on the Sino-Cuban Friendship Commune outside Beijing.

Each production team[31] had a clinic, with a larger health centre at brigade level in the nearest large settlement, 15 minutes away (2.5 km) from the clinic, again by bicycle. Patients unfit to cycle or walk came to his clinic by jeep, of which the commune had several. The one we saw was an army vehicle.

The doctor was also responsible for training medical auxiliaries who carried first aid kits to the fields when they went to work. One of his jobs was basic hygiene propaganda, to discourage spitting and smoking, and to persuade people to sterilise water before drinking it. He said intestinal diseases were the most common complaints, followed by inflammation of the lungs, larynx and bronchial tubes (presumably due to smoking as the local air quality was good).

He added: 'Children's diseases are mostly stomach upsets. Tapeworms are very rare and we have no children with swollen stomachs.' Although he was aware that acupuncture could be used for anaesthesia, at the clinic they only used it 'as a therapy'.

'Farm work is very healthy.'

We then had a long talk, about daily life for an 'ordinary' commune family, with a woman, introduced as a 'housewife', who told us foreign visitors used to be 'very few'. Our interviewee (whose name I didn't record) said she had three children, aged six, three and one. The older two were in the kindergarten, which was open from 6 a.m. until 10 a.m., when the mothers stopped work, and again from 3 p.m. until 7 p.m., while the mothers worked their second shift of the day. Her youngest child (who regarded us with rapt astonishment, as the picture shows) had been ill recently but there had been no serious childhood diseases in her family.

Organic and low-tech: a traditional, locally-made wheelbarrow used for muck shifting at the Sino-Cuban Friendship Commune.

She had only a primary education but her husband finished middle school. They both did general farm duties and worked in the fields: 'Farm work is very healthy.'

'Before Liberation we had only one room. Now we have a three-roomed, bricks-and-mortar house built by ourselves.' There was no rent and no charge for water supply.

The joint income of the husband and wife was about 800 yuan[32] per year (67 yuan a month). Of this they had about 300 yuan left in cash after meeting the costs of rice, other grains and electricity: 'Expenses here are different from in the city.'

They had a private plot on which they kept 10 hens and two pigs (which were sold to the State). They grew about 600 catties (about 300 kg) of grain for the family: 'The output of

---

[31] A production team was a group of households, often several hamlets.

[32] About the same income as the barefoot doctor in the same village.

grain per mou[33] before Liberation was about 100 catties. Now it's about 1,000 catties per mou,' she said[34]. They also grew beans. Her family had three meals a day. She cooked about 6 catties (3 kg) of grain a day[35]. Meat was not eaten every day. They bought one large portion of meat a week. 'The children have eggs every day as the hens lay five or six every day,' she said.

The furthest our interviewee had travelled was to Beijing: 'The city is where we go on holidays. We either take a bus from the bus stop 1.5 km away or there is a train station very near. Young people use bikes for exercise. On our visits to Beijing the family get their photographs taken.'

They also bought clothes in town but more than 60 members of their production team had sewing machines. She bought her own sewing machine in 1970 'outright for cash' not on hire purchase. The family also had a transistor radio which we were asked to admire. Their furniture was all purchased, none of it made by the family. On a shelf were books - selections of Chairman Mao's works and some books on agriculture, lent out by the production team.

Piglets at a farm on the Sino-Cuban Friendship Commune.

We heard that celebrations were held on 1st May, 1st October, New Year's Day and 8th March, International Women's Day. There were regular film shows in the commune by travelling projector teams.

Musical performances and recreational activities were organised by production team members. Twice a week the production team had 90 minute meetings to study political thought. Our host also spoke about marriage customs: at a wedding there was an evening meal for friends and relations, with candles and cups of tea: 'They sing a few songs and there is free talk,' she said.

A Scots delegate snaps the piggery at the Sino-Cuban Friendship Commune near Beijing. There was hardly a fly in sight as the pens had been sprayed with insecticide. As with the duck farm, production was on a much bigger scale than on the old family farms.

---

[33] A *mou* is 0.067 hectares = 0.165 of an acre, or 666.5 square metres.

[34] This statistic, like most of those supplied by the Chinese Communist Party at that time (and often since), was questionable. She had presumably been given it by the local Party boss.

[35] That adds up to roughly 1,000 kg a year, so by her account the family was producing about a third of its carbohydrate requirements from the private plot. Not many British allotment holders could match that.

In the production team she said they had 'a special family planning group making propaganda'. What was the best size for a family? In her family there were two sons and one daughter 'so the mother is very pleased'. The most appropriate age for a woman to marry was 25 to 27. Her mother and father were 21 and 28 respectively when they got married.

Although this meeting was obviously carefully planned, the woman did appear keen to answer our questions frankly. She certainly had a positive attitude, pointing out the undeniable improvements in the lives of working people since her own childhood, but she didn't lecture us on Maoist doctrine as the Revolutionary Committees often did. In fact she didn't mention Chairman Mao or his thoughts once. She was thus far more effective than the officials in giving foreigners a good impression of China. That may be why the local Party boss selected her to talk to us.

Beijing ducklings' raised at the Sino-Cuban Friendship Commune.

Nicely fattened and ready for the table: Beijing ducks at the Sino-Cuban Friendship Commune.

Waiting to welcome the 'honoured foreign guests' at the Sino-Cuban Friendship Commune.

Unidentified fibres (possibly flax) drying at the Sino-Cuban Friendship Commune.

Although just a few miles from China's capital city, horse-drawn carts and muck spreaders were still in widespread use on the Sino-Cuban Friendship Commune.

More of the intermediate technology: a horse-drawn cart with a home-made slurry tank bolted onto a timber chassis. Sino-Cuban Friendship Commune.

Secondary school students from Beijing finding out about 'the life of the broad masses' on a work party at the Sino-Cuban Friendship Commune. 7th September 1972.

On the crumbling Great Wall

On Thursday 8th September we had a day off, with a very jolly bus trip from Beijing to the Great Wall of China. We did not interview a single Revolutionary Committee member, all day long. Considering how famous the Wall was, it was a surprise to find only a few dozen other visitors there. Most were Chinese, with a few flight crews from foreign airlines and scattered groups of 'honoured foreign guests' on tours like our own. There was a short section where we could walk along the top of this astonishing barrier and imagine the barbarian hordes kept at bay (or sometimes not) in earlier centuries, but the wall on either side of this was derelict and crumbling. The authorities had not yet worked out how much foreign exchange the Wall could bring them if they marketed it properly as a world heritage destination.

Every tourist, then as now, had to see the Great Wall of China. This section had not yet been renovated. 8th September 1972.

Back in Beijing we attended an evening performance of *The White-haired Girl*, one of only eight 'revolutionary' operas approved by Madame Mao as she sought to stamp out all traditional opera, theatre and music. Despite this it was a most polished and enjoyable performance, albeit somewhat melodramatic for Western tastes. Based on a traditional tale, it was first performed in 1945. By 1972 over 120 million Chinese had seen a film version of the show. The plot was complicated, particularly if one didn't understand Mandarin, but the story was simple: in the bad old days of feudalism women had a particularly miserable time of it (which few would deny) but all ended happily thanks to the Liberation. As with *The Red Lantern* opera that we'd seen in Guangzhou, the message was: Mao Zedong good; Kuomintang bad. They didn't miss a trick, these Party ideologists.

A scene from a more recent production of 'The White-haired Girl'. Photo: China Daily/Wikipedia.

Not really a university?

Next day we were back on the Marxist treadmill with a lengthy visit to Beijing University.

The main gate of Beijing University today. Photo: Wikipedia.

This was where the Cultural Revolution had begun in 1966, with a single 'big character poster' criticising the university authorities, culminating in an insane orgy of false accusation, bullying, torture, murders and suicides. The chaos had closed the university, and most of China's other institutions of higher learning, for four years. Eventually even Mao and his fellow gangsters Liu Shaoqi and Lin Biao had had to send in the army to restore order. But then Mao sent most of the students away to the countryside to 'learn from the broad masses'. In reality this usually meant living in squalor on starvation rations while the army exploited them in its labour camps or the peasants upon whom they were billeted shunned and resented them. Only in 1970 did the universities re-open but two years later most of the students had not returned from internal exile. Some would never do so. Many were dead. Many more had lost their right to return to the cities. The full horror of what was done to a generation of Chinese students is told in Frank Dikötter's book. What we heard at Beijing 'University' on 9th September 1972 was a sanitised travesty of the truth. But we didn't know that at the time because one of the things the Chinese Communist Party is really good at is public relations and we were being deceived (in the most charming manner, of course). One of those exiled students was the future emperor Xi Jinping, the son of a senior official. The official, heart-warming story of his time 'learning from the broad masses', if true, was certainly not typical.

None of this was mentioned in a lengthy interview with the Beijing University's Revolutionary Committee, which had 39 committee members:

> 9 teachers
> 7 students
> 3 workers
> 6 Chinese Communist Party cadres
> 7 Army propaganda team
> 6 workers' propaganda team
> and one 'family member' (whose role and selectorate were unexplained)

Each of the 17 departmental Revolutionary Committees had a similar structure:

> Liberal Arts   Chinese History
>   History
>   Philosophy 'etc.'

Languages	Western languages
	Oriental languages
	Russian Literature
Sciences	Maths
	Physics
	Chemistry
	Biology 'etc.'

Although this committee structure seemed unwieldy, and undoubtedly was, it appeared on paper to be more representative of the university's staff and students than the Edinburgh University Court over which I had presided as 'Lord Rector' since my election by my fellow students the previous year. However, the Beijing version was clearly an echo chamber for the Party line, not a debating chamber. At least we were allowed to disagree and vote in the Edinburgh University Court Room at the Old Quad, even if the membership included the Principal's personal physician, two law lords and only two student representatives (who, with the junior staff, were routinely outvoted by the establishment).

The Revolutionary Committee chair gave us a potted history of Beijing University: it was founded in 1898 as Peking Normal College, to train court officials of the imperial dynasty; at that time 'all the students were from the landed classes'. During the Warlord and Kuomintang periods it 'continued to serve the ruling class'. This much was undoubtedly true. Much the same could be said for Edinburgh, where the governing body, while encouraging poor 'lads o' pairts' with bursaries and scholarships, had been very slow to admit women students, particularly to the Medical Faculty.

Unlike Edinburgh, Beijing University had a history of revolutionary activity. Mao himself was a librarian there in 1918 and again in 1920. According to his biographers he felt the academics and students looked down on him as a country bumpkin[36]. This probably fuelled his intense contempt for intellectuals, or indeed for any serious form of intellectual activity beyond the study of classical Chinese literature and the writing of poetry.

Beijing University was the cradle of the May Fourth Movement for republican democracy in 1919. In 1949 it was 'handed back to the people' (i.e. to the Chinese Communist Party). In 1952 there were 'new adjustments' to all higher learning institutions.

So we can date when it ceased to be a university in the sense understood by Western academics: 1952. The Revolutionary Committee would not agree, of course, but after that year it became increasingly difficult, and ultimately impossible, for teachers or students to make honest, independent inquiry into the history of their country, to debate the merits of competing political, social and economic theories, or to question the pickled orthodoxy of Marx, Engels, Lenin and Stalin, as interpreted by their self-appointed evangelist, Mao Zedong in his 'thoughts'. This could be said of almost all Chinese institutes of higher

---

[36] Mao had a pronounced Hunan accent which would have been considered uncouth by mandarins in imperial China.

learning but we were told that Mao took 'a personal interest' in his *alma mater* and had 'given instructions on teaching reforms'.

In other words, the 'university' had become merely an instrument for the Communist Party's indoctrination and control of intellectuals and professional specialists.

We then received this account of the Cultural Revolution:

In 1966 the Big Character Poster campaign was the start of the Cultural Revolution, when 'the broad masses were mobilised' in mass criticism of Liu Shaoqi's 'revisionist line'. There was 'a split in mass organisations after this campaign', with 'fist fights' and a 'battle with all kinds of weapons'. The archival and oral history sources quoted by Yang Jishen, Frank Dikötter and other writers have established that there were numerous instances of harassment, torture, wrongful imprisonment, murder and suicide in and around the campus.

None of these crimes was mentioned in our interview with the Revolutionary Committee, nor the fact that the army suppressed the Red Guards on the campus in 1967. However, our informants did say that in July 1968, Mao sent in a 'worker-peasant propaganda team' to 'lead the Cultural Revolution' and they 'reconciled the two factions' and 'exposed a few bad people' who had 'hidden in mass organisations'. More reliable historians have seen this as Mao's attempt to deflect criticism and place the blame on others for the tragedy that took place in this former seat of learning and civilisation, and in others throughout China.

In September 1969 the Revolutionary Committee was established and there had since been 'a process of educational reform'. Teachers and students 'went to the countryside and factories to learn from the workers'. In my ignorance I noted this down without asking how and why it happened. What we heard from the cloned drones on the Revolutionary Committee was a gross euphemism for the gigantic, cruel and utterly destructive internal exile of millions of blameless students and of citizens with 'bad backgrounds'.

It seemed the agony had all been worth it for, when the 'university' eventually re-opened its doors in 1970 the first enrolment of students since the Cultural Revolution was 'quite different from previous students'. Just as we'd heard at Dongshan Medical College in Guangzhou, before the

Big Character Posters at Beijing University, 1967. Photo: Wikipedia.

71

Cultural Revolution admission was by entrance examination, for middle school pupils only. The minimum education standards for admission were now junior middle school[37].

Back then there had been 'no contact with workers and peasants'. So, the story went, 'then' was bad; 'now' was better:

- Enrolment now was *[preferentially]* from 'those with practical experience'.
- Students had to be physically in good health and 'politically in good health'.
- Before a worker or peasant applied for admission there was a 'mass discussion' followed by a 'mass resolution' in the applicant's production team or workshop.
- Then came approval by 'the leadership of local organisations' where 'we must guard against problems of favouritism and nepotism'.
- If the worker/peasant had worked for five years prior to being admitted as a student then he or she continued on full pay, with tuition, medical charges, lecture fees, board and lodging all paid for by the State.
- Other students (i.e. those going to university from school, or who had worked less than five years before applying to study) got an allowance from the State.

The requirements were almost identical to those we'd heard about at Dongshan. Similarly, Beijing had brought in 'reform' of teaching content, materials and methods, to implement and combine theory and practice. As with the relaxation of entrance requirements, these reforms sounded reasonable to listeners from the West, where for years we'd been hearing about the gulf between the liberal arts and the sciences and how it was wrong that technical colleges were still the poor relations of prestigious and well-endowed universities.

In the Science Faculty students worked in small scale factories within the university, as well as in big factories outside, where they could 'learn from the workers'. This seemed admirable but then we came to the Liberal Arts Faculty, where they studied 'Marxist-Leninist works, Mao's works and history'. They also studied 'bourgeois works for comparison' (although not, of course, for emulation): 'The practical work for them is the whole society'. Later, at Fudan University in Shanghai, we would discover that a novice lecturer in the Economics Department had no knowledge of major Western writers on his subject.

We were assured that 'negative and imperialist works' were studied at Beijing, as well as officially approved writers. In the Philosophy Department, for example, students studied Plato, 'although not in detail' and they were aware of Bertrand Russell, who was included in 'contemporary bourgeois philosophers', given credit for his 'critique of modern revisionism' and his opposition to the Vietnam War, but criticised for his 'idealism'.

In English language teaching the emphasis was on oral work, using a small tape recording laboratory: 'Grammar is not neglected but not over-emphasised'. Fair enough;

---

[37] In Scottish terms, that meant fourth formers could go to university as well as sixth formers.

grammarians have been in headlong retreat in most English-speaking countries since at least 1972.

The new teaching methods sounded good: 'In the past there was cramming and spoon feeding, like the force feeding of Beijing duck. Now teachers use the method of enlightenment, stimulating students' initiative.' I wondered, but did not ask, if this admirable principle extended to studies of Marxist-Leninist philosophy and Maoist politics.

Lecture sheets were distributed for study before classes: 'Then there is discussion with the students, who are free to correct other students and teachers.' This I also doubted, having witnessed the craven conformity of the Revolutionary Committee, but no doubt they knew it was what we wanted to hear.

On the topic of examinations we heard (the academically unsuccessful) Mao's famous opinion trotted out again: 'In the past teachers made surprise attacks on students. Teachers were the enemies of students. Now they help students to review their lessons and to check their programme of teaching and study.'

The speaker continued: 'There are oral and written tests. The questions are distributed in advance for study and discussion... Special attention is given to creative answers of students. If a student's answer is not creative but merely a copy of the teacher's ideas then they get ordinary marks... Some memorising is still necessary...

'There is a comradely relationship between teachers and students at periodic discussions to assess study and teaching ability. Teachers and students criticise each other openly as part of mass assessment of teaching and study. Teachers still set exam papers and give marks. A group of teachers do the marking.'

So, despite the Cultural Revolution, they had not found a way to get rid of 'surprise attacks on students'. As in Guangzhou, we heard: 'This is an experimental phase of reform. There are still some difficulties.'

Students might indeed encounter some 'difficulties' if they took this teaching policy at face value, I thought (to myself, for by now it was clear that all questions requiring an answer that departed from the prepared script would only produce another chunk of Maoist cant). For example, if students really did openly criticise a teacher who was a Mao loyalist or questioned a point of Marxist orthodoxy, albeit in a 'comradely' way, the recent experience of millions of their contemporaries suggested that they ran the risk of expulsion, internal exile, prison or even death. In such circumstances it might be suicidal to attempt 'creative' discussion on alternatives to Mao's policies. In retrospect, I did not realise how terrified our interviewees must have been during these staged encounters: as late as 1972, a single wrong word could cost you your job, your freedom or your life.

Significantly, 50% of the staff in Political Economy were Chinese Communist Party members, whereas in Biology, a less politically sensitive subject, only 40% of the faculty were in the Party. The mere fact that such statistics were kept by the 'university' proved, to me, at least, that it wasn't one. But at least they did not keep (or did not share with us) statistics on Party membership among students. At that time there were 20 million Party members in China, which had a total population in 1972 of about 871 million[38], of whom about 500 million were adults entitled to vote. So the proportion of Party members among university teaching staff was about ten times higher than the 4 or 5% in the general adult population. This underlined the Chinese Communist Party's determination to keep intellectuals under tight control.

We then asked about rates of pay, which seemed a safer topic. Staff salaries appeared to be set nationally, because the figures quoted for Beijing were similar to those in Guangzhou. There were 13 grades for university teachers, ranging from 56 yuan to 340 yuan per month[39]. Other university employees earned from 30 yuan to about 100 yuan per month (for skilled workers). Only 10% of employees earned the highest rates. We were assured there would be wage increases 'soon' for the low paid workers and (of course) this was 'quite different from the USSR'.

We discussed the relationship between university degrees and highly-paid jobs and received the usual bland, official answers. A committee member said the theory was 'to each according to his labour' but there were still some highly paid bureaucrats. The wage system was 'going to be changed' but 'you cannot simply abolish high rates of pay'. The problem was 'related to the policy for bourgeois professors'. There was 'a need for a united front' and we were reminded that such people were very few: 'In the past 10 years the number of highly paid people has remained stable or has decreased. Wage increases will only be for the low-paid.' (If this was the case, I wondered, why had the Cultural Revolution not managed to do anything about it?)

The university had teachers from all over China, some with postgraduate experience: 'Some veteran workers and peasants have been here as teachers since the Cultural Revolution, also engineers and technicians from outside and some research personnel from the Chinese Academy of Sciences.'

This sounded fine but then we learned that before the catharsis of the Cultural Revolution there had been 'some' postgraduate students but now there were 'none'. The official figures were 4,300 undergraduates[40] and 2,200 teachers. This extraordinarily high student/staff ratio confirmed the scale of disruption to higher education caused by the Cultural Revolution. In September 1972 Beijing University's student body was less than half the size of Edinburgh University's – and a tiny fraction of what you would expect if Beijing University had student numbers in the same proportion to China's total population as Edinburgh University had to Scotland's. The Revolutionary Committee

---

[38] That is the official figure now given for the 1972 population. At the time, we were told it was 760 million.

[39] This seemed an extraordinarily high number of grades but may have been a hangover from the days of the mandarins.

[40] This figure is probably wrong. There were at most a few hundred Beijing University students in 1972, according to Dikötter. We saw no more than a few dozen when we had lunch in the canteen and walked around the lake on campus.

spokesman said the plan was to build up student numbers to 7,000-8,000 and later to more than 10,000.

The Chinese Communist Party also took great care to control the Students' Union which organised academic, cultural and sports activities as well as 'political study and propaganda'.

Students could 'put up nominees' for the union's Revolutionary Committee which was 'elected by hand' after 'mass consultation' but there were no secret ballots: 'Leading comrades have the final decision'. Back in Edinburgh, our leading Maoist and Trotskyite student comrades (and there were a few) would never have stood for that sort of undemocratic nonsense.

Asked about relationships between male and female students, a Red Guard at the meeting at first said there were 'no restrictions at all' but then added that men and women students were 'not allowed to live together' and 'boys must not be admitted to female students' residences during rest hours' (i.e. overnight).

It appeared from this that Chinese traditional morality was undiminished by the Cultural Revolution and, unlike some other traditions, might even have been strengthened, although obviously not for Chairman Mao and his harem.

So how did this Revolutionary Committee, in the place where the trouble had started, explain the Cultural Revolution? It came about because of 'the masses' dissatisfaction', according to a Red Guard committee member who had been on campus long before 1966. His reply was essentially the same as we got everywhere else when we asked this question but it is worth recording as an example of the distorted accounts fabricated in Mao Zedong's history workshop, where facts always mattered much, much less than his latest Party line:

> 'The Cultural Revolution was a continuation of the struggle against the Kuomintang, the proletariat against the bourgeoisie.

> 'Liu Shaoqi was not alone. It was not just an individual struggle. In Tianjin Liu Shaoqi raved, glorifying the exploitation of the workers by capitalism. He urged the development of capitalism in China and preached that class struggle was dying out. He even suggested the break-up of the proletarian dictatorship[41].

> *[Further examples of the alleged perfidy of Mao's old comrade and one-time nominated successor were recited, at some length].*

> 'In July 1958 Mao's call for proletarian education had a warm response in the university. All Philosophy Department teachers and students went to a nearby commune to do farm work and social investigations. This line was opposed by the educational hierarchy who tried to sabotage it. An inspection by the Education Minister criticised the teachers and students for not reading books. He tried to stop our experiment.

---

[41] He did nothing of the kind, of course. He just thought peasants should be allowed to sell produce from their private plots and handicrafts made in their spare time. But Liu Shaoqi, like the rest of the Party bigwigs, had form in purges and mass murder so perhaps we should not feel too sorry for him.

'In 1960-62 Liu Shaoqi exploited the situation. He criticised the Philosophy Department line of 1958 as disorderly and confined students to campus.

'The Cultural Revolution was preceded by a teacher and student boycott of revisionist education. We criticised the elitism of capitalist-roaders. Some worker-peasant students were expelled by Liu Shaoqi's bureaucracy. They said 'We love Beijing but we hate Beijing University'. Many were dissatisfied with so-called academic freedom and the dissemination of reactionary theories. For example, in 1958 one university teacher started a course in Hegel's philosophy: he introduced Hegel objectively but the teacher was personally influenced by Hegel. He almost eulogised Hegel[42]. Worker-peasant students criticised this policy. Their criticisms were ignored.

'On 16th May 1966 the Chinese Communist Party decided to carry out a Cultural Revolution. This was the origin of the Big Character Poster at Beijing University.'[43]

I then asked if the Red Guards' policies had been achieved. Another Red Guard replied:

1. They had consolidated the proletarian dictatorship.
2. It was a victory. Liu Shaoqi was defeated.
3. As a student here before the Cultural Revolution she was not guaranteed enough time for political study. There was no restriction on this now.
4. There was now more enrolment of workers and peasants. Although she was from a worker background herself she had found herself being influenced by the Liu Shaoqi line.
5. She was not fully satisfied with the results of the Cultural Revolution but not disappointed because the class struggle would continue.

Mao Zedong and his then deputy, Lin Biao, in Tiananmen Square with Red Guards, 1966. Photo: Wikipedia.

---

[42] Georg Wilhelm Friedrich Hegel (1770 –1831) was a German philosopher whose ideas about the importance of the self and of religion Marx and the Communists rejected.

[43] The Red Guard may have slightly lost the plot here. We had earlier been told that the first Big Character Poster *preceded* the Party's decision. But perhaps this was just another example of Mao's infallible hindsight...

Snake and dog for dinner

After this long session with the ideologically correct bigots of the university's Revolutionary Committee (reminiscent of 17th century New England Puritans, who also had their revealed truths, sacred texts and relentless intolerance of dissenters) we were indulged by the China Travel Service with a sumptuous banquet of innumerable courses in a high-ceilinged dining room within the Great Hall of the People.

Of course, I felt guilty at tucking into such a spread (the snake and dog were particularly delicious) when I knew the workers and peasants back in the Da Li People's Commune would only be having a bowl of rice for their supper, but I felt I'd earned a treat after a weary day taking notes of fossilised cant in a university that in 1972, as far as the liberal arts and social sciences were concerned, wasn't really a university at all, just a sad, slightly scary brainwasheteria.

The Great Hall of the People today. Photo: China Travel Guide.

Perhaps emulating Chairman Mao's famous Yangtze swim, a citizen goes for a dip in Kunming Lake below the Summer Palace, Beijing. 10th September 1972.

A row on the lake

We were back to sightseeing next day when we enjoyed a fine view of Longevity Hill as we were rowed slowly around the beautiful Kunming Lake to see the Empress Dowager Ci Xi's famous marble boat – the 'Boat of Purity and Ease' – at the imperial Summer Palace. The weather was warm and the excursion extremely agreeable. The water did not look that clean but many of the younger townsfolk were

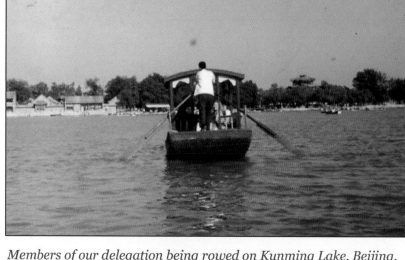

Members of our delegation being rowed on Kunming Lake, Beijing. 10th September 1972.

following Mao's example and swimming briskly, pausing only when confronted by the astonishing sight of two boatloads of foreign devils.

Pleasure boats on Kunming Lake, Beijing, with not a lifejacket in sight.

Our last call in Beijing was at the zoo, to see the sad, captive pandas – imprisoned by iron bars rather than by the ideological shackles that bound the Chinese citizens who'd come to gaze at them. I have always found zoos depressing. This one was no exception.

On our visit to the Beijing Zoo this disconsolate panda wasn't doing much; but then pandas don't do much in the wild either.

The Yangtze Bridge in the rain

On the evening of Saturday, 10th September 1972, the Scotland-China Association study tour boarded another slow train for the 600-mile journey to Nanjing, the former capital. We saw little of the provinces of Hebei and Shandong as they passed slowly in the darkness. But we did see that many people's houses had electric light, which very few would have had in 1949.

It was raining at noon the next day when we crossed the huge, double-decker road and rail bridge over the Yangtze at Nanjing. It had been completed only four years earlier and, while not as beautiful as our own Forth Rail Bridge, it was a symbol of Chinese self-reliance and national pride. Gu Shu Bao suggested I take its picture. If I did, I have since lost the slide, so here is a more recent snap by someone else (taken in similar weather):

The First Nanjing Yangtze River Bridge. Photo: Juan Gutierrez Andres/Wikipedia.

Our first stop was the Sun Yat Sen Mausoleum which, to give the communists their due, credited Dr Sun's leadership of the 1911 'bourgeois' revolution that overthrew the Qing Dynasty. Sun could not be airbrushed out of history, for everyone knew that Mao Zedong had, long ago, been an ardent youthful disciple of the former Kuomintang leader who was (briefly) China's President. Sun Yat Sen, however, wanted a democratic future for his country, freed from foreign colonisers. Although he was a bit of a Han supremacist, he would have been horrified to see the emergence of a dictatorship and Mao's cult of personality. The museum displays presented him as a 'forerunner' of Maoism, which was true, but not in the way that great Chinese patriot and democrat had envisaged.

In the evening we saw a performance of revolutionary songs and dances by children of the 'Little Red Soldiers'. It was wonderful to behold but you had also to wonder, and feel slightly uncomfortable, at the extreme regimentation and severe discipline that must have lain behind such flawless singing and dancing by such very young children.

Celosia cristata (Cockscomb) bloom in the garden of the Sun Yat Sen Mausoleum, Nanking. 11th September 1972.

80

At school in Nanjing

The following two days were spent mostly in schools. The Chinese Communist Party was rightly proud of its achievements in education. Almost all children had access to a primary school, even in remote rural areas, and the majority to high school – at least 'junior middle school' level. Large numbers went on to senior middle school and to colleges and universities. At all levels of education there was a strong emphasis on acquiring practical, useful skills. This was a vast improvement on the situation before 1949 and a far cry from the elitist system under the Qing Dynasty. But I found myself wondering, as we visited a Nanjing primary school, did a Chinese classroom really have to look so austere and regimented, just like the one I remembered from my first day at school in an Oxfordshire village back in 1952? And was all this learning by rote really the best way to help pupils to learn?

Poster poem in a Nanjing primary school. It reads, in part:
'Little bits of white cloud over the mountain tops,
'Layers of soft fields covered in green foliage,
'Poor and middle peasants learn from Da Zhai [the famous model commune]...'

Part of the answer was financial: the barracks-like brick classrooms with their spindly desks and chairs were extremely basic simply because the country did not have enough money for anything warmer, better lit, more airy and better equipped. Well, perhaps it did, but the demands of the national military budget, particularly the nuclear weapons programme, appeared to take precedence over better school buildings. Even so, children were now in school whereas previously they would have gone out to work at the age of eight or even younger. That was a great transformation.

The other part of the answer was that the intrinsic nature of written Chinese dictates the amount of memorising required. I'd had enough trouble learning just 26 letters of the alphabet in that Oxfordshire schoolroom when I was five years old. Arabic looks very difficult to an English reader but in fact has just two

Practising her characters in a Nanjing schoolroom.

more letters than we do. Hebrew has only 22 in its 'alef-bet' but, as in Arabic, they are all consonants. Learning our alphabets is a walk in the park compared with what these young Nanjing scholars faced: they would have to memorise a minimum of 2,000 characters before they could be called literate in Chinese. To be considered an educated person they would need to recognise about 8,000 characters, even in the simplified system introduced after 1949, and in total there were at least ten times that number of Chinese characters in the average dictionary. It was a daunting prospect for a young mind but no-one had yet found a better method than rote learning in endless classroom choruses under the gaze of a stern disciplinarian.

The sad thing was that learning by rote also seemed to be the way most other subjects were taught. And of course the method was ideal for memorising political slogans and inculcating the ideology of Mao, the 'Great Helmsman'. Admittedly, chanting political slogans did seem to help the Lu Xun Middle School pupils to keep almost in time while doing calisthenics at their PT class in the school playground.

The indoctrination was pervasive and, to our Western eyes, depressing but there were also school workshops where all students, not only classes of 'non-academic' boys, learned basic craft and mechanical skills, including even welding and operating lathes. Was it justifiable that the products from the school workshops were sold in aid of public funds?

That moment every pupil in the world dreads...

Was this, in effect, ⟨...⟩
were they just obeying ⟨...⟩
'serve the people'?

The emphasis on education was certainly ⟨...⟩ normal practice in Scotland ⟨...⟩ time, where most secondary education was still segregated by gender, selective at 11 or 12 years of age (to say nothing of the sectarian divide between Catholic and Protestant) and actively discriminated in favour of an academic elite, to the detriment of what Mao would have called 'worker-peasant' pupils. When I was at school in England in the 1950s, pupils who couldn't pass the '11+' tests went to

An astronomy lesson in a Nanjing junior middle school.

'secondary modern' schools for the 'non-academic', marked for life as less valuable people. This deplorable system still exists in some English counties.

Lathe turner and senior pupils, Nanjing. 13th September 1972.

Keeping fit in the playground. Nanjing. 13th September 1972.

Mercury on the floor

Our last call in Nanjing was to a mercury switch factory in some shabby, ill-ventilated shacks where school pupils sometimes went for work experience. Our hosts were extremely proud of it. The Revolutionary Committee chair explained that Mao Zedong Thought had helped former manual workers to learn the special skills required for this delicate work. That may be so, but it was clear that occupational health was not a priority of the management committee. The workshops were downright dangerous, with visible spillages of mercury on the workbenches and floor and almost certainly traces of mercury vapour in the air. The whole operation was in flagrant breach of even the 1972 health and safety standards in the UK and most Western European countries.

Flower in a public park, Nanjing.

Slogan on a wall in the garden of our hotel, Nanjing. It reads, in part: 'The proletariat and oppressed peoples of the world unite!'

Wuxi: the Grand Canal city

The city of Wuxi lies on the Grand Canal in the lake country west of Shanghai. For me it was the highlight of our trip, with several fascinating visits in a place that looked like Venice before mass tourism. As in so many of China's ancient cities, many of the interesting and picturesque old buildings have since been destroyed by brutalith blocks that sprouted like fungus during the bizarre era when China embraced rampant capitalism and called it 'Socialism with Chinese characteristics'.

We were housed in a large and very beautiful guest house, then being renovated in traditional style on the shores of a beautiful lake. I suspect it was for very senior cadres and we were the first foreign guests to have stayed there. The view over Tai Lake to the distant hills was idyllic. This too has been destroyed, the guest house by a hideous Marriott hotel and the view by a motorway and a snaggle of not so distant skyscrapers.

The Grand Canal in the centre of Wuxi.

The view of Tai Lake from our guest house, long since obliterated by a peculiarly ugly and tasteless Marriott chain hotel. 14th September 1972.

A new footbridge for the pleasure of senior cadres and honoured foreign guests in the exquisite gardens of the Tai Lake Hotel.

Barges on the Grand Canal. Often compared with Venice, Wuxi has had similar problems with floods.

What 'Socialism with Chinese Characteristics' has done to the Grand Canalscape of Wuxi: a frontage of picturesque canalside houses is all that remained in 2022. Photo: Wuxi tourism website.

A backwater canal in Wuxi in September 1972.

In 1972 Wuxi looked much as it always had, the only signs of modernity in this picture being the concrete sampan, the power line and the wall poster exhorting the citizenry to greater efforts.

A creek leading from Tai Lake into the city of Wuxi, 16th September 1972: a view now dominated by tower blocks and motorways.

A boat makes the daily inspection of a Tai Lake fish trap.

Traditional arts and crafts

The Mao cult was still all-pervasive in September 1972, with larger-than-life statues of the communist emperor prominently displayed in every town and city. Most private houses also had a small plaster bust of the Great Helmsman but there were signs that other, less overtly political, artistic subjects were becoming more popular.

On arrival in Wuxi we were taken to a small factory where they were churning out plaster figurines of sturdy peasants in regional costumes, as well as pandas by the thousand. There seemed to be more of these than of Mao. Perhaps pandas were outselling him?

Plaster of Paris busts of Chairman Mao were still a big-selling item at the figurine factory we visited, but sturdy peasant girls were just as popular. Wuxi, 14th September 1972.

Tedious, repetitive and finicky work: painting plaster pandas all day, all week, all year...

Artistic inspiration: evening on Tai Lake from Two Hills Park, Wuxi.

Art for art's sake?

There was obviously a latent demand for traditional art that by no stretch of the imagination could be said to be 'serving the revolution'. In a side room of the figurine factory we met two charming elderly gentlemen, extraordinarily skilled artists who were masters of the traditional style. They were painting meticulous pictures of birds, flowers and mountain scenery, with not a distant, red-flag-waving column of Long Marchers in sight. So Chinese art in classical style was no longer the preserve of the wealthy elite but now accessible to the broad masses. And perhaps not everyone really agreed with Mao that all art must be political. Some things were just beautiful.

Wuxi ferro-cement boat factory

On our first morning in Wuxi we visited a canalside factory where they were making sampans out of ferro-cement. A shortage of timber made these economic, even though they were heavier than the traditional craft. They were also harder-wearing, longer-lasting and needed fewer repairs.

The boatyard's Revolutionary Committee were a cheerful crew, as well they might be, for here was a concrete example (if you will

An upturned hull ready for the cement pour.

pardon the pun) of what workers' ingenuity and self-reliance had achieved. It was a success story. Harry Dickinson was fascinated and asked many technical questions before we were taken for a short cruise in a newly launched sampan on the Grand Canal to round off a memorable morning.

Turning a finished boat prior to launching.

The painstaking job of fixing the wire mesh for a deck section of a ferro-concrete sampan. Wuxi, 15th September 1972.

Poling the finished product to the fitting-out dock.

Spreading the cement mix on the hull of a concrete sampan.

Scotland-China Association delegates float testing a newly launched sampan.

A modern ferro-cement barge delivering timber to a Wuxi boatyard. 15th September 1972.

A corner of the Wuxi docks. The barges are mostly of timber construction but cargo is lifted by labour-saving electric cranes into the waiting trucks, carts and railway wagons.

Awaiting the helmsman: the rudder department of the Wuxi boatyard.

Ho La Commune, Wuxi

In the afternoon, at the Ho La People's Commune in the suburbs of Wuxi, we had another wonderful time. Here the commune idea really seemed to be working, which is probably why we were taken there. The commune's 15,000 inhabitants were not only managing to feed themselves (not too difficult in peacetime in this region of rich soils, a mild climate and plentiful water) but they also had several productive sidelines:

- silkworm rearing;
- an embroidery workshop;
- fish pond management and harvesting;
- pearls from farmed shellfish.

An elderly peasant takes a keen interest in what the Revolutionary Committee chair is telling the foreigners. Ho La Commune, Wuxi, 15th September 1972.

Mao's principles in action: this well-staffed cobbler's workshop made sure the commune was self-sufficient in footwear. Ho La Commune, Wuxi.

The people we interviewed at Ho La were all friendly and frank. We did not feel we were being deceived. There was a very good atmosphere in the village we visited, perhaps not surprising in view of the relative prosperity the commune had created for its members.

If all the communes had been like this they would probably have survived Deng Xiaoping's reforms in the early 1980s. However, the very prosperity of the more successful communes may have undermined them. It was clear that many of the peasants and workers we met on this and other model communes had considerable personal savings. The lack of consumer goods for them to buy with their savings was putting pressure on the centrally planned economy, which was unable to deliver.

Another Maoist principle of the 'Great Leap Forward' – diversify! A shellfish farmer inspects the lines. Ho La Commune.

Paradoxically, some recent economic studies suggest that the Maoist principle of self-reliance, admirable as it appeared to some at the time, had seriously disrupted traditional trade routes and markets. Sometimes it was better to allow a large factory to specialise rather than encouraging lots of smaller, less economic ones.

There had always been a secret economy running parallel to what was allowed to happen officially, with 'black markets' in a wide range of goods and services. It was the black market that had saved millions from starvation during the economic chaos of the Great Leap and the Cultural Revolution. And, as the Chinese Communist Party would discover in the years after Mao, unlicensed dealers, itinerant hawkers and street traders could stimulate the economy and respond to consumer demand much faster and more efficiently than state economic planning committees.

There were some marketable pearls in this unfortunate bivalve. Ho La Commune.

Former rich peasant's farmhouse, Ho La Commune.

Technology old and new at the Ho La fish ponds

Dozens of large fish ponds were another source of income and food for the workers at Ho La Commune. The fish were fed on vegetable waste and pig manure.

A traditional, hand-operated quern for grinding up grains and beans for duck and fish food. Ho La Commune, Wuxi, 15th September 1972.

No shortage of labour as the boats netted the contents of a fish pond.

An electric mill to replace the labour-intensive quern. Ho La Commune. On many communes in 1972 electricity was provided free by the state.

Curious toddler, Ho La Commune.

The carp that got away: 'Never mind, it'll be bigger next time,' the fisherman said.

Modern housing and canal boats. The message on the gable end is: 'Serving the People'.

Vernacular farm buildings with tobacco plants (right). Ho La Commune.

Rice paddies and vegetable plots watered by an irrigation channel that also served as a canal for boats bringing weed and silt for fertiliser from Tai Lake. Ho La Commune, Wuxi, 15th September 1972.

The Red Detachment of Women

Returning from Ho La, in the evening we attended a performance in Wuxi of the dance drama *The Red Detachment of Women*. This was a new version of an old story, based on a famous 1961 film that the Red Guards had condemned as 'counter-revolutionary'. The tale was simple enough: a unit of women soldiers had played an important part in the revolution but their story and their martial achievements had then been forgotten. In the film they were portrayed as heroes but the truth was more complicated: their detachment only lasted half a year before the women were defeated by the Kuomintang. Taken prisoner or going into hiding, they were often labelled as 'anti-Party' elements by the Party and treated very badly. Here were echoes of Stalin's treatment of Soviet soldiers taken prisoner by the Nazis and imprisoned as 'traitors' on return to their homeland. I was not able to understand exactly how the plot of *The Red Detachment of Women* film had changed in this melodramatic stage version but it seemed to be aimed at rehabilitating them. Whatever the historical facts, of course, the fact that this version had the approval of Madame Mao and her censors was all that mattered.

Much more interesting, for me, at least, was a visit next morning to a silk-reeling factory in Wuxi. I knew nothing about silk other than it somehow came from silkworms. The guided tour was a revelation. We had seen silkworms being fed with chopped mulberry leaves grown on Ho La Commune but now we saw how their cocoons were unravelled and turned into thread in an extremely complex process involving a great deal of skilled but repetitive labour.

Going to work at eight years old

The chair of the Revolutionary Committee, Chaoshu Long, told us her personal history. Her husband worked for the telephone company in Wuxi and was formerly in an electrical factory. They had two children, aged five and three, who attended the nursery school in the factory. Chaoshu Long had started work in the silk mill at the age of eight, one year before Liberation.

Her father was a hired hand in the countryside. Her mother was also a silk reeling worker in the mill:

> 'In 1948/49 I only worked seven months here. All our parents' earnings could not support them and their family of five children. So I had to go to work aged eight.

More Maoist diversification: worker feeding silkworms with chopped mulberry leaves grown on the commune. Ho La Commune.

103

I had no schooling. I couldn't recognise my own name. After Liberation there was a night school in the mill, where I learned to read and write.

'In 1954 I joined the Communist Youth League. With the help of the Party and veteran workers in 1958 I became a cadre in charge of the youth league but not divorced from work – it was only in my spare time. In 1960 I joined the Chinese Communist Party. Since the Cultural Revolution I was proposed by the workers to [be on] the Party Committee in this mill.

'Comparing before and after the Liberation, the sky and the earth were turned upside down. My family had been looked down upon by politics and economics. At supper we didn't know where breakfast would come from. After Liberation, women were politically and economically emancipated.'

This was true but we had noticed several times that although Chinese women were legally emancipated and entitled to do what was formerly only men's work they still seemed to do most of the child-rearing and domestic chores, a pattern familiar to 'liberated' women in the Soviet Union (and elsewhere). Nonetheless, women like Chaoshu Long had every reason to believe in the Party and to defend it against Mao's enemies, real or imagined.

A work party of girls, probably high school students, learning about the dignity of labour by helping with renovations at Wuxi station. Their labour is unlikely to have been wholly voluntary but at least they were living in the city. Millions of teenagers were still exiled in the countryside at this time.

Tai Lake, Wuxi

On Friday, 16th September, a day of perfect weather, our hosts laid on a delightful afternoon boat trip around the Tai Lake, one of the natural wonders of China. This was not only for us to admire the beautiful scenery of the ninety or so islands but also to demonstrate the significance to the Wuxi economy of China's third biggest lake.

A fleet of fishing boats, mostly propelled by traditional, battened sails, made a picturesque composition for the photographers. These rickety-looking vessels, some of them clearly very old and patched, were landing large tonnages of freshwater fish, crabs and other shellfish every year, adding to the impressive harvest of carp and other farmed species from the fish ponds we had seen on Ho La Commune. Other boats, generally smaller and even more ramshackle, were dredging for silt and gathering floating weed, all to be used as organic fertiliser on commune fields.

This all seemed admirably self-sufficient and sustainable but disaster was lurking under the surface. Already in 1972 there was considerable run-off from fields, fish ponds and city sewers into the lake, slowly but surely building up pollution by nitrogen fertilisers and increasing the biological oxygen demand.

Caryl Robertson and the author enjoying a beer and a free cigarette on a Tai Lake boat trip, 16th September 1972.

Traditional sails hoisted as the fishing fleet sets off for a night's work. Tai Lake.

A Tai Lake boat crew heading home with a load of waterweed for use as organic fertiliser on commune fields.

In the last two decades of the 20th century there was a vast increase in industry around the lake shores. The human population rose accordingly. In a single year, 1983, it was estimated that a billion tonnes of wastewater, 450,000 tonnes of garbage and 880,000 tonnes of animal waste were dumped in the lake, which was the water supply for 30 million people. The national authorities started a campaign to clean up Lake Tai and set a target date for compliance with water quality standards. The deadline passed and on

New Year's Eve 1999 Beijing ordered almost 130 factories around the lake to close down. Things got a little better but serious pollution remained.

In the summer of 2007 there was a massive algal bloom and much of the lake was poisoned by cyanobacteria, killing fish. Beijing declared an official 'natural disaster', denying it was caused by human activity, but then ordered another 1,300 factories around the lake to cease operations. A conservationist campaigner, Wu Lihong, was sent to prison for three years for publicising the ecological catastrophe and, allegedly, threatening polluters. On his release in 2010 he claimed that in fact none of the industrial plants had been closed down.

Commune workers gathering weed and silt for organic fertiliser, Tai Lake

Another attempt to clean up the lake, by Jiangsu provincial authorities with the State Council's backing, had failed by 2012. Efforts continue today but Lake Tai is still polluted by agricultural fertilisers, sewage and industrial effluent, including heavy

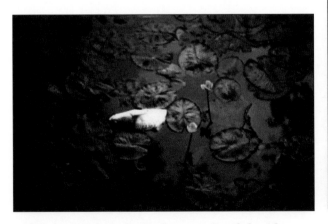

A fish succumbs to lack of oxygen in a lakeside pond, Wuxi. 16th September 1972.

Laden to capacity with waterweed, a Tai Lake workboat heads for home.

metals, oily waste, agricultural pharmaceuticals, pesticides and microplastic particles. The same can be said for many other lakes in China, where the dictatorship of the Communist Party has proved to be an environmental disaster. The same can also be said for many other countries' governments, of course, but in China the problem is compounded and aggravated by the censorship of inconvenient truths and the absence of independent news media.

New pavilions in traditional style at Two Hills Park.

A family afloat on Tai Lake. 16th September 1972.

Evening at the Two Hills Park pagoda.

Wuxi and Tai Lake in 2022. Photo: M. Rahman/Wuxi tourism website.

To Shanghai, formerly the fleshpot of Asia

It was only about 70 miles from Wuxi to Shanghai but it seemed to take much of the day to get there. It was a Sunday so perhaps the trains were even slower than usual. After the beauties of Wuxi the big city was drab but still fascinating. There were few traces of its failed notoriety as Asia's most sinful city between the First and Second World Wars. The Peace Hotel where we stayed still towered impressively over the Bund but the few bright lights remaining on the mostly undistinguished buildings downtown were advertising Mao, not consumer goods.

We were now very near the mouth of the Yangtze so in those car-free days the traffic jams were on the water, not the streets. The Huangpu, the Yangtze's winding tributary that runs through the city centre, was thronged with sampans, barges, river steamers and ocean-going ships. Some of us walked along the Bund and through a woodland park to Suzhou Creek, where we bumped into some seafarers from the Gambia at the Bar of the sailors' home. I'd wanted to see 'Soochow Creek' because my Uncle Peter told me he enjoyed a 'run ashore' some 20 years earlier when he was a British Merchant Navy deckhand, not long after the Liberation.

It was raining at noon the next day when we crossed the huge, double-decker road-and-rail bridge over the Yangtze, just north of the city centre. Nanjing is about 200 miles from the ocean but even so its... ...beaches... From our bridge, we saw... symbol of a Chinese... ...suggested I take its picture. If I did, I have since lost the slide, so here is a more recent snap by someone else (taken in similar weather):

The First Nanjing Yangtze River Bridge. Photo: Juan Gutierrez Aguado/Wikipedia.

Our first stop was the Sun Yat Sen museum which, to give the communists their due, credited Dr Sun's leadership of the bourgeois revolution that overthrew the Qing Dynasty. Sun could... ...for everyone knew that Mao Zedong had, long ago, been a... ...of the former Kuomintang leader who was (briefly) China's President... ...however, wanted a democratic future for his country, freed from foreign colonisers. Although he was a bit of a Han supremacist, he would have been horrified to see the emergence of a dictatorship and Mao's cult of personality. The museum displays presented him as a forerunner of Maoism, which was true, but not in the way that great Chinese patriot and democrat had envisaged.

In that China, we saw a performance of revolutionary songs and dances by children of the ... Soldiers. It was wonderful to behold, but you couldn't help but wonder, and feel slightly uncomfortable, at the extreme regimentation and severe discipline that must have lain behind such flawless singing and dancing by such very young children.

Wooded parkland at the west end of the Bund, looking upstream over the Huangpu at its junction...

Suzhou Creek in 2020. Not much of the woodland survives. Photo: Shanghai city tourism website.

Celosia cristata (Cockscomb) bloom in the garden ... Dr Sun ... Mausoleum, Nanjing, 11th...

Shanghai, 11th September 1971. Here is a huge ... communications tower about to be hoisted to the vertical. Many of the traditional buildings have since been levelled to make way for the gleaming downtown of modern Shanghai.

Next morning we were kept busy with a hectic programme including a housing estate, a primary school, a lightbulb factory run by 'housewives' and an old people's reading room. Interviews with the Revolutionary Committees at each location followed the now familiar and mind-numbing formula: Mao Zedong Thought had helped overcome all obstacles.

View looking downstream from the Peace Hotel. September 1972.

The housing estate visit reminded us that although most country dwellers[44] in China were owner-occupiers, many city people were tenants of the municipal authorities or housing co-operatives. Private landlords were, of course, outlawed, although some property owners (mostly with 'bourgeois' antecedents and thus classed as having 'bad backgrounds') were allowed to share their homes with extended family members[45]. Most of the splendid Shanghai mansions, built in the late 19th and early 20th centuries by foreign business managers and local gangsters, had been converted into government offices or subdivided into flats. Although conditions in the new and converted blocks of flats were hardly luxurious they were far better than the tarpaper shacks where many of the Shanghai working class had lived before Liberation. In 1972 there were still privately owned tenements in Scotland's cities that were in a worse condition than the estate we

Looking upstream from the Peace Hotel, 2022. Photo: Shanghai city tourism website.

---

44 At that time roughly 80% of the nation's households were classed as rural and engaged in agriculture.
45 In Beijing the family of Mao's doctor, Zhisui Li, were among them – until their home was requisitioned by the state during the Cultural Revolution.

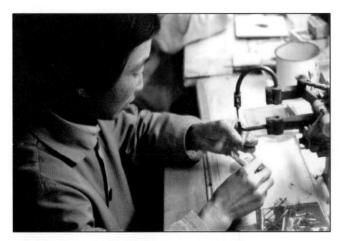

Assembling lightbulb filaments, Shanghai.

saw in Shanghai. In China, as in most Scottish towns, the authorities made sure there was a primary school within easy walking distance of the pupils' homes.

The lightbulb factory provided much-needed employment to a few dozen married women in the district but here again the Maoist principle of decentralisation and local self-sufficiency brought a contradiction, straight out of the 'bourgeois' economist Adam Smith's 'pin theory': the lightbulbs they produced so laboriously and inefficiently in the tiny factory (of which they were so proud) were obviously never going to be able to compete with large, modern lightbulb factories producing much greater quantities of higher quality goods for sale over a vastly greater area. In 1972 the Shanghai housewives didn't have to compete. Mao had seen to that, but I doubt if this little social enterprise survived Deng's reforms and the unleashing of the market economy.

I mentioned earlier that we had a 'bourgeois' economist with us, Professor Radha Sinha of Glasgow University, and these points did not escape his notice. Radha firmly believed in basing his research on solid data. Early in our tour he'd realised that some of the statistics we were given by Revolutionary Committees were inflated or imaginary, particularly when talking about crop yields. So, while other members of the party visited a hospital, Radha and Harry spent the afternoon on one of Shanghai's main shopping streets, collecting raw, reliable data on the prices of food, clothing, shoes and consumer goods such as thermos flasks, alarm clocks, radios and bicycles. Many of the statistical tables in Harry's final report were based on Radha's meticulous data collection. But, as with most economists (including his Chinese contemporaries) Radha's attempts to put his local findings into a broader national picture were hampered by the Chinese Communist Party's cavalier approach to collecting, analysing and publishing accurate facts and figures. Like history, facts and figures were primarily tools for propaganda. If a fact didn't fit the Party line, it became a non-fact.

A fire engine passing secondary pupils marching to school along Beijing Road, Shanghai. 18th September 1972.

Barges, houseboats and ferries on the Huangpu River, Shanghai. 17th September 1972.

Just a few miles from Shanghai city centre, a traditional Chinese rural scene of houses, ducks and boats on a canal at the First of July Commune.

The glorious First of July

There were more economic statistics to collect when we spent all the next day at the July First Commune in the suburbs of greater Shanghai. July the First is celebrated as a national holiday on the supposed anniversary of the founding of the Chinese Communist Party in Shanghai (by Chen Duxiu and Li Dazhou, not Mao Zedong[46]) in 1921. The first congress, according to records from the Soviet Union (whose agents sponsored it) actually started on 23rd July 1921 but because of a police raid the delegates fled seven days later, leaving important documents behind them, and later re-convened elsewhere. But July First Commune is easier to say that July Twenty Third to Thirtieth Commune and who needs facts anyway?

This was another very impressive showpiece commune of over 16,000 inhabitants, slightly larger than Ho La (14,820 inhabitants) in Wuxi but much smaller than Da Li (63,000) outside Guangzhou. The main crops were grain and vegetables. Like all the other communes we visited, it was not far from the city and so there was a ready market for fresh produce.

Traditional timber houses in a village lane on the First of July Commune, Shanghai. 19th September 1972. Although picturesque, these dwellings were often insanitary and always a fire hazard. Since 1972 most of them have been replaced by blocks of flats.

Our itinerary did not include any communes in more remote areas and again this should be borne in mind. We were undoubtedly seeing some of the most successful examples. In some areas away from the densely populated regions we visited there were still considerable food shortages and even destitution and sporadic, localised famine in September 1972. Again thanks to writers such as Yang Jisheng[47] we know this now, but few knew it then and the Party was not about to volunteer such embarrassing information.

At July First, however, all seemed to be going well. We saw a bright, cheery primary school where the pupils sang songs for us and chorused 'Good morning!' in English. We met their parents in agricultural machinery workshops, a small factory making furniture for local

---

[46] Mao was still an enthusiastic supporter of the Nationalist Kuomintang at that time.
[47] See Yang Jisheng, 2021, *The World Turned Upside Down – a History of the Chinese Cultural Revolution.* Swift Press (revised version of first Chinese edition published in 2016 by Cosmos Books, Hong Kong. ISBN 978-1-80075-085-2).

use and an electric motor assembly plant, where the same economic contradiction appeared as in that Shanghai lightbulb factory the day before.

Imported Friesian dairy cows, First of July Commune.

Here we saw our first Chinese dairy cattle, Friesians imported from the Netherlands. The Chinese are traditionally not keen on dairy products, mainly because most Han are lactose intolerant. I don't think we saw cheese or yoghurt anywhere on our travels, but we were repeatedly told that young children had access to milk and that seemed to be the case. The dairy sheds were beautifully clean and the cows looked contented, or as contented as any dairy cows can be under a regime that, of necessity, always involves some cruelty and stifling of instinctual behaviour.

The Revolutionary Committee showed us pig, chicken and goose-rearing farms, a mushroom growing section, an ingenious underground irrigation system and rice paddies that also grew a crop of wheat in rotation. Harry was particularly delighted by the machinery workshops and the 'low-tech' efforts to mechanise agriculture. The commune's blacksmiths and welders were making new ploughs and harrows, repairing old equipment and even replacing timber and stone ploughshares on traditional oxen-drawn wooden ploughs with new, steel ones.

Interpreter Gu Shu Bao with a traditional timber plough, brought to the workshop to have a new, solid steel ploughshare fitted in place of the old wooden one. First of July Commune.

We saw several designs of wheelbarrow, all of them appearing easier to handle than the standard British farmyard barrow (but perhaps that was just the skill of the Shanghainese barrow boys). We met the tricycle van again, and I was allowed to drive the pickup version, watched anxiously by Mr Chen.

The author, minus his Mao jacket, road-testing a Shanghai-made tricycle pickup.

Our interpreter Mr Chen (left), Harry Dickinson and the driver of a two-wheeled 'walking tractor' hitched up to a trailer on the First of July Commune. The machine had a single-cylinder engine with fuel tank mounted over the gearbox and a simple, open-topped radiator tank above the cylinder. When the engine got too hot you just poured more water into the tank and it boiled off. The belt drive looked lethal.

Steel ploughs, harrows and rollers, many of them made in the commune workshops.

We had a close look at the ubiquitous eight-horsepower 'walking tractor' with its horrendously dangerous unguarded drive belt and an open-topped radiator, from which boiling water spouted intermittently. The machine could be hitched up to a cart for general transport as well as doing its main job of rotavating the fields.

The mechanics in one workshop proudly displayed a Chinese-made version of a Czech 35hp tractor. In another, skilled carpenters still made traditional wooden buckets and storage bins but, of course, everyone wanted modern, steel buckets that were lighter and longer lasting.

Traditional, locally made wooden buckets still in daily use.

From discussion with the Revolutionary Committee it was clear that, although the commune farmers made every effort to maximise the use of organic manure and composts (the new cowsheds being a handy source of additional nutrients), they were starting to use relatively large quantities of artificial fertilisers and were aware of the pollution hazards from excess nitrogen runoff. They were also worried about the potential ill-effects of pesticides and herbicides, but apparently not worried enough to stop using them.

Gu Shu Bao at the wheel of a Chinese-made tractor. It appeared to be a copy of a Czechoslovak machine.

'A very miserable life'

We interviewed several families on the July First Commune including seven members of one family, including a grandmother and sister and brother-in-law who lived with them. The mother remembered:

> 'Before Liberation we led a very miserable life. My father was a farmhand for the landlord. My parents had 12 children. I was the ninth one. The three youngest died. It was very hard to feed the children. There was not enough to eat or to wear. Since Liberation our standard of living has been greatly raised. Now we have enough food and clothing.'

Her husband was a docker. Her elder brother worked in a farm tools and machinery plant, her sister-in-law on the commune's livestock farm. She and her mother did manual work around the commune. Only Granny and the young nephew stayed at home.

The family's total income was some 270 yuan per month, similar to the average

Chopping up pumpkin gourds for animal fodder. First of July Commune.

115

we had recorded at Da Li and Ho La communes:

'My husband earns 70 yuan; my brother and sister-in-law 90 *[between them]*; Mother and I earn from 60 to 70 yuan *[between us]* and there is some income from sidelines, such as crocheting lace, so *[the total is around]* 270 yuan. Some people work full-time knitting. Some do crochet in their spare time.'

The Mother of the family appeared to be the banker, as we had heard elsewhere. Members of the family gave her money for food. There was a personal allowance for food and they kept the rest themselves. However, there was no regular payment to Mother and the arrangement seemed *ad hoc*.

Each family had a private plot of 0.07 *mou* per person so with seven people in the household their plot was 0.49 *mou [326.5 square metres]*. They grew soy beans, egg plants and Chinese cabbage. They were self-sufficient in these vegetables and had a surplus for feeding hens and pigs. They had no pig at present but 33 chickens... and three ducks.

We also heard details of their surprisingly low monthly outgoings:

- They paid no rent as the house was owned and was built by the family itself just 20 years ago [1952]. Electricity cost them only 1 yuan and 20-40 cents a month. Running water was just 30 cents per month. The commune supplied half of their fuel for cooking and heating. The family bought the other half, including some coal *[150 jin per month = 75 kg]*. Their six-monthly fuel bill came to about 1 yuan 80 cents a month.
- Medical insurance was free for her husband, her elder brother and her sister-in-law as they were all in regular work. For her, the grandmother and the nephew the cost was 1 yuan 50 cents a year each.
- Expenses for clothing and bedding for the whole family were about 10 yuan a month.
- Spending on entertainment was at most 5 yuan per month, including bus fares to town: 'Granny and I go to the commune cinema once a week, the younger ones twice a week. And also to the opera. Tickets are often only 5 cents, the maximum is 15 cents.'
- On Sundays and holidays there were 'invitations and visiting'. She visited her elder sister in town and sometimes they came out to the commune to eat with them.

She said the family had three meals a day, two of rice and one of gruel. Every day about 6 jin (3 kg) *[of grains]* for the whole family: 'We're self-sufficient in vegetables and have plenty of eggs – four a day. We buy pork and fish from town. We buy meat three times a week and fish three times. Once a week we buy eggs. Only the child has milk, half a pint a day from the commune farm, also gruel from age 10 months, also milk powder.'

Our interviewee had two elder brothers, one working in Anwei province and married to a Shanghai girl who was a primary teacher. One of her three sisters, a member of staff at the Shanghai teachers' college, was visiting the day we spoke. She told us about her life. She was 23 and said she was 'too young' to marry. She took part in local political meetings and meetings twice a week in her production team, once a month in the youth section, once in the general section. There was a monthly meeting of the Communist Youth League in the brigade and also militia meetings but these were not regular. The furthest she had been from the village was Kiangsu province, last month. She planned to travel a little and would like to go to Hangzhou. Her mother went to Anwei last year to see family.

Asked which countries in the world she thought were friendly to China, she gave a diplomatic reply: 'As Chairman Mao says, people of the world have friends all over the world. US imperialism is our enemy but we make a distinction between the US people, who are also our friends, and their government.' Did she want to stay in the countryside? More diplomacy: 'Wherever our motherland needs me most.' This young woman had heard of Scotland before we arrived. She was the first who told us this!

In the evening, on our return to the Peace Hotel from the July First Commune, there was considerable excitement when a nearby tenement building caught fire. The fire brigade was quickly on the scene and it seemed there were no casualties.

Another 'university' of wilful ignorance

The following morning, while other members of our group visited a school for deaf mute children and saw acupuncture treatment in progress, I accompanied Professor Sinha to Fudan University, where we were to interview a young economist whom I shall call Comrade Tong. He had graduated in 1970 and worked in a factory for one year after that, being 're-educated by the workers'. Although on the faculty he had not done any teaching yet. He had a special interest in Japan and was studying the language.

He told us the Fudan University's Revolutionary Committee was set up in late 1967 (two years before Beijing University's) and had 'about 31' members, including members of the Workers' and Peasants' Mao Zedong Propaganda Team, plus representatives of students, staff and Party cadres. There was also a smaller Standing Committee which presided over the Revolutionary Committee proper.

Tong said that in 1967 the chairman and vice-chairman were both students. Another vice-chairman was a worker specialising in electric lighting. After two or three years the student chairman and vice-chairman graduated and went elsewhere. They were Red Guards, not Party members. A propaganda team arrived at that time and some workers became Revolutionary Committee members. In late 1970 the first batch of 1,200 students were admitted, on the same proletarian conditions as in Beijing. Some were elected as members of the Revolutionary Committee.

One of the propaganda team was currently acting chairman. Another worker was a vice-chairman and a Party cadre was the other vice-chairman. Tong had no information on the present Party membership status of the individual Revolutionary Committee members and did not appear to be a member himself. Some students were still on the Standing Committee.

My eyes were glazing over so I asked about pay grades. He said that since 1963 there had been no staff promotions. The distinctions of rank that existed, after the Cultural Revolution, were as follows:

1. Assistant Teacher;
2. Lecturer;
3. Assistant Professor;
4. Professor.

However, within that list there were 12 different pay grades (almost exactly the same as we had found at Beijing) ranging from a 'top grade professor' on 370 yuan a month down to a 'third grade assistant lecturer' on 60 yuan and a recent graduate on probation earning up to 50. Students got 20 yuan a month, as elsewhere. This system was at present under 'reconsideration'', perhaps awaiting a decision by the next Party Congress. Tong was appointed by 'the State', not the Revolutionary Committee.

How much personal choice was allowed in job allocation? He replied that 'within the general plan' for the allocation of graduates to jobs, the graduate's own preferences were taken into account in 1963. The situation was the same now.

During the year before the Cultural Revolution began, he had studied:

- History of the Chinese Communist Party;
- Political Economy;
- Economic History of other countries (USSR, USA, France, UK);
- Accountancy;
- Foreign languages (Russian).

He mostly concentrated on the USSR. There was no study of Third World countries.

Tong took part in the Cultural Revolution and afterwards did not resume his studies, only 'a bit of Marxist-Leninist theory of political economy'. This had included:

- *Correct Handling* by Mao Zedong;
- *Imperialism* – Lenin;
- *Wages, Prices and Profits* – Marx;
- *Anti-Duhring* – Marx.

He had never heard of Engels' book *Wage Labour and Capital*. He had read Volume One only of *Das Capital*, but of that only the parts covered by the lectures. He read most of these books by himself, before the Cultural Revolution.

He was currently reading *Critique of the Gotha Programme* and *Socialist Upsurge*. He also read Western economists, or ˉid before the Cultural Revolution, and was preparing to teach Ricardo, Adam Smith, J. S. Mill, Malthus and Keynes. But he had never heard of Joan Robinson or J. K. Galbraith, appeared to know nothing of modern Western economic thought and had no wish to know.

The suggestion that students might critically examine Marx or Mao was emphatically rejected. We concluded that our interviewee was an orthodox conformist, interested only in received Maoist wisdom. But that may just have been for safety's sake, with our interpreter present. Hopefully he broadened his learning later in his career. For now, as we left the Fudan University building Professor Sinha just shook his head sorrowfully at this spectacle of wilful ignorance and dogma being rewarded with a post at an institution of higher learning.

Electrical progress

Welding work at the Shanghai No 1 Turbo-generator Factory. 20th September 1972.

After lunch we re-joined Harry Dickinson, who was in his element on a visit to the Shanghai No. 1 Turbo Generator Factory, an hour's drive outside the city. There we saw assembly of various generators of up to 300 megawatts. This was impressive, considering the low state of Chinese electrical technology before the Liberation, and the Revolutionary Committee was keen to point out that the achievements in this field had happened despite the withdrawal of Soviet technical assistance 12 years before. We also visited the plant's day nursery and interviewed workers in their homes on a nearby housing estate. Later there was more heavy engineering at the Shanghai Industrial Exhibition. To remind us who was taking the credit for China's industrial achievements, a gigantic statue of Mao Zedong dominated the main hall.

上海工业展览会大厅
The main hall of the Shanghai
Industrial Exhibition

Arrested in Shanghai

When we got back to Shanghai the China Travel Service, which had our passports in its possession, informed us that there'd been a miscalculation in the office and we'd have to pay twice the agreed price for the trip. I felt a twinge of panic. There was no way I could possibly find such a sum. How many years in a re-education camp would I get if I didn't cough up? Somehow this was all sorted out, shortly after Harry Dickinson and I had been arrested. I believe some of our party paid up later on. I didn't, not only because I couldn't but also because I thought it was an attempt at extortion. I sometimes wonder what happened to the China Travel Service official who miscalculated the price. Nothing nice, I suspect.

It was while we were at a performance by the astonishingly skilful Shanghai Acrobatic Troupe that evening that Harry was delighted to bump into an old acquaintance, the British engineering trade union leader Hugh Scanlon, sitting in the row behind us with none other than the celebrated Canadian-born economist J. K. Galbraith, who invited us to come back to his hotel for a drink after the show, to compare notes on our respective itineraries and impressions so far. We agreed and later that evening, as Harry and I left the Peace Hotel[48], strolled up the Nanjing Road and entered the Beautiful River Hotel, I was thinking of where I might sell an exclusive interview with the world-famous Professor Galbraith, sharing his thoughts on China's communist experiment. In the lobby of the Beautiful River Hotel Professor Galbraith was waiting and greeted us warmly. But, before our order for drinks could be taken, armed police intercepted us and, ignoring the pleas of the celebrated author of *The Age of Uncertainty* and other learned works, cancelled our planned *soirée* and firmly escorted us to a police van. Again I had visions of a decade or so in the slammer but fortunately the van took us straight back to our own hotel, not to the jail. In *A China Passage*, his book about his visit, Galbraith mentioned our brief encounter at the theatre, but not the detail of the police involvement.

Disappointingly, in this amusing little volume (much of which he seems to have written on the plane home) Galbraith would join the ranks of gullible Westerners who gave generous praise to Mao Zedong's achievements in agriculture and industry, despite remarking that Chinese Government economic statistics were either unreliable or unavailable to scholars (including Chinese scholars) or even non-existent. Like me and most of our Scottish delegation, he was too ignorant and too polite to inquire closely about the 1958-62 famine which was caused, not by bad weather as Mao claimed, but by the forced collectivisation of farming and his insane 'Great Leap Forward'. In fairness to the professor, even as late as 1972 very few people outside China were aware of the scale of that catastrophe a decade earlier. I certainly wasn't. Nor did Galbraith dwell on the economic and personal calamities of the Cultural Revolution. It had destroyed the careers, and in many cases the lives, of Chinese intellectuals who no doubt wished to enjoy the

---

[48] Now the Fairmont Peace Hotel. Many Shanghai hotels have changed their names since 1972. The hotel where Galbraith stayed was off the Nanjing Road and was probably the luxurious palace now known as the Grand Central Hotel, greatly altered and refurbished.

same academic freedoms as the famous Harvard professor of economics. After visiting just a couple of them, he acclaimed China's 78,000 People's Communes – almost all of which had to be closed down, by popular demand and Communist Party fiat, just 10 years later, making way for the revival of Chinese agricultural production after Mao's ruthless and cruel experiments in social engineering. But hindsight is a wonderful thing...

From our own hotel window the next morning we had a superb view of Shanghai's factories belching black smoke on the horizon – and of the street below, teeming with bicycles and pedestrians, not cars. Almost all of the very few cars we saw in China 51 years ago belonged to senior Communist Party cadres or to the People's Liberation Army. Our interpreters had not long been released from detention during the Cultural Revolution (which, we now know, did not really end until Mao died, four years after our trip) – their crime was being 'intellectuals' who could speak English. Gu Shu Bao appeared terrified that he might end up back in a punishment brigade. He was dreadfully upset by our unauthorised excursion to meet J. K. Galbraith and I felt ashamed for letting him down. His colleague, Mr Chen[49], seemed less agitated about it.

'Educated youth' learning from the peasants in the countryside. A page from the Shanghai guidebook produced for Nixon's visit in 1972.

[49] Always referred to just as 'Mr Chen'. I suspect he was more senior than Gu Shu Bao and Chang Mao (whom Chen had replaced after we left Chang with John Chinnery in the Guangzhou hospital).

A private conversation

Carl and Paul[50] Crook were two students, the sons of David and Isabel Crook, mentioned above, who worked in a Beijing agricultural machinery factory. Our discussion in Shanghai on 21st September 1972 lasted three hours and was the last major interview of the trip.

Paul Crook (2nd from left, back row) and workmates in Beijing, about 1970. Second from right is probably his brother Carl. Photo: BBC/Crook Family Archive.

The Crook boys just happened to be on holiday in Shanghai when we arrived there, as did Rose Smith, whom we'd already met in Beijing. An astonishing thing, coincidence. Even more astonishing, to me, at least, was that during a long interview about industrial relations, pay and conditions in the factory where they worked, neither Carl nor Paul mentioned that their parents had been arrested on trumped-up charges or that when we met them their father was still in prison almost five years after his arrest, usually in solitary confinement without the right to family visits or even correspondence[51].

The encounter was of particular interest because they spoke to us in English, without interpreters present. So, unlike almost everyone else we met in China, what they said could not be reported back to Chinese Communist Party security goons via the China

---

50 Paul Crook's life story is told on the BBC web page https://www.bbc.co.uk/news/magazine-15063195

51 There is a statue of David Crook in Beijing, where in 2019 Isabel was awarded the Friendship Medal, the highest honour a foreigner can receive in China, presented to her by Xi Jinping in person. See: https://www.fmprc.gov.cn/mfa_eng/topics_665678/zggcddwjw100ggs/jszgddzg/202208/t20220830_1 0757630.ht ml

Travel Service. They appeared to speak frankly despite not mentioning their parents' appalling treatment during the Cultural Revolution. Perhaps it was a test, to see if Carl and Paul would complain to the Western visitors about their parents' persecution, and whether we would publicise the injustice after our return to the West. We, of course, were completely unaware of it, as were most people, inside and outside China.

We began by sharing impressions of our visit and they 'corrected some mistaken ideas' about 'contradictions' in the workplace on the road from socialism to communism. For example, as we had noticed in our visits to universities, there were still wide disparities in wages. They argued that simply increasing lower pay would take far longer and cost far more than the relatively straightforward method of reducing higher salaries unilaterally. The argument that there were only relatively few highly paid people was used to claim that a reduction in their pay wouldn't be worth the fuss. But the fact that the very highly paid (the 250-350 yuan-per-month class) were not all that numerous was in fact the best argument for the practicality as well as the necessity of cutting their pay.

They reported that traditional Chinese deference to authority persisted, not least in the Chinese Communist Party hierarchy. This deference could take the form of fear of authority or of respect for the persons occupying responsible positions.

Even after the Cultural Revolution there were no fewer than 27 levels of Government cadre. For example, all university graduates automatically became 24th grade cadres whereas work brigade leaders were 15th or 16th level cadres (presumably Mao was 1st grade – I didn't ask).

Before the Cultural Revolution there were eight grades of worker in their factory:

- Grade 1 were apprentices and new workers who automatically rose to Grade 2 after two years;
- Grade 3 was sometimes automatic or could be a progression based on skills;
- Grades 4-8 were originally based on the development of the worker's skills.

This grading system was almost universal in Chinese factories but promotion according to skills was now being 'reconsidered' and appeared to have ceased in the brothers' workplace, where the highest paid worker was an American technician earning 300 yuan a month.

They explained what they understood by the phrase 'democratic centralism'. According to Mao's theoretical writings, 'the masses' should make suggestions to the leaders about policies, nominations for posts of responsibility, working conditions and pay. The leaders should then make a decision but it should come into effect only after approval by the masses. What actually happened was that the leadership did consult the masses but the masses didn't have the final say in the selection of candidates – the cadres did. This appeared to us the very negation of democracy but we heard that in practice there were moderating factors.

It was said to be very rare for the leadership to reject a nomination by the masses. This was because either the masses knew who'd be acceptable to the leaders or because the leadership did as it was told by the masses. At present, the latter seemed to be the most frequent situation.

'If the masses do decide to get rid of a cadre they have the power to do so.' There had been two examples of this in the Crook brothers' factory in recent months.

There was 'mass criticism' of an unpopular manager. He was defended by a friend of his on the People's Liberation Army (PLA) in the works. The PLA man addressed a meeting and tried to cool the situation. However, the manager was eventually dismissed after the workers made use of the fact (or the allegation) that he was having an affair with a member of 'the May 16 Organisation'. 'May 16' was a very popular bogey – it was quite possible that it didn't actually exist[52] although the brothers said they knew people who'd been accused of belonging to it, a sort of secret society associated with everything bad, from Liu Shaoqi on the right to Lin Biao on the left.

In another case a new PLA man was sent by 'above' to the factory: at a mass meeting things became very boring and the workers began to drift away; the PLA man became very angry and gave them a lecture on socialist morality; he demanded that group leaders immediately take the names of the absentees, in order that the PLA man could dock their pay (meetings officially counted as work time). There was no response from the group leaders. Eventually the PLA man had to name team leaders personally and demand that they do this. Again there was a stony silence. He repeated his orders. Reluctantly, the Crook brothers' group leader (a much respected comrade) stood up and looked around him: 'All right, you lot! Hands up those who've skipped off.' Nonetheless, the PLA man got his way and pay was docked from the absentees. Paul's group, with six out of 20 absent, escaped thanks to the obstinacy of their team leader.

'The PLA man was technically in the right because meetings were work. The workers were morally in the right for upholding their right not to attend badly run and boring meetings. It wasn't their fault that meetings were badly run.' Eventually this particular PLA man was removed after pressure from the workers about his dictatorial behaviour.

We then heard about the Cultural Revolution and the abolition of work bonuses. To some extent this was tokenism and only the name had changed. In their factory, at least, bonus was abolished and the lower paid got a rise – but deductions were then made from the pay of workers who didn't attend meetings or whose work didn't come up to the standard or who went absent without leave. Thus a very similar system to bonuses continued to operate. Only those who worked as hard as they used to work for the bonus were entitled to the new, higher rates of pay at the full value. The workers were well aware of the subtleties of this and took an attitude of cynical amusement to such bureaucratic semantics.

We were told: 'Bureaucracy was always bad before the Cultural Revolution and still persists despite it.' Workers did take part in management but those selected tended to become part of the bureaucracy themselves. In the Crooks' workplace there was some

---

[52] It was indeed a figment of Mao's imagination, as we now know, invented for the purpose of undermining his opponents in the Chinese Communist Party.

popular resentment on the shop floor about the snootiness of Communist Party cadres. They did eat the same food as the workers but they tended to congregate in their own corner of the mess hall. Most workers did not grudge the cadres their extra remuneration (in this factory only about 10 yuan a month extra, at most) and in general the cadres did not enjoy significant special privileges. The resentments were about personal and social behaviour rather than purely economic differentials.

As for the PLA, they said we should know that four pockets in the uniform tunic signified that the wearer was a company commander and above (sometimes a platoon commander), while two pockets were for the lower ranks. Those wearing epaulettes and shoulder straps (for holding the uniform cap when it wasn't on their heads) were very important persons. They said there was general respect for the PLA, despite the dislike of some self-important new recruits, and 'it really is different from other armies'.

To further clarify the hierarchy of the people's democratic dictatorship, we heard this explanation: 'The Militia are not the people one sees in what look like blue PLA uniforms – they're police. The white-uniformed traffic cops are also 'security police' – checking movements of vehicles and individuals, checking passes and permits, etc., and keeping an eye on 'undesirable elements'.

'The militia don't have a uniform. They wear what they like, even on manoeuvres with the PLA. They're the local guerrilla-type force. The division of labour between blue-uniformed and white-uniformed police is not clear, apart from traffic duties. There are also plain-clothes police. If there is a secret police it is so secret that no-one knows about it.'

Precisely, I thought.

What was really going on?

After this interview, and other conversations with Western expatriates (including Rose Smith) in which we had attempted, without success, to discuss Lin Biao's flight and Liu Shaoqi's alleged 'capitalist roaders', I made the following contemporaneous notes on what I thought was going on in China in September 1972:

Left Opportunism (LO) and Right Opportunism (RO) are both considered deviations from the 'mass line', as dictated by Mao, and therefore seen as equally reactionary in their historical effect.

The difference may be this: Right Opportunists are those who actively work for a less 'socialist' society – a 'return to capitalism', meaning a return to private small enterprise and a large measure of personal incentives i.e. a social democratic/mixed economy with a strong, centralised bureaucracy, little decentralisation of industry and commerce, and little local 'democracy'.

ROs also wish to slow the pace of 'socialist education and construction' (i.e. Maoist indoctrination) because, while sharing the Chinese Communist Party's ideals of a communist society, they are less optimistic about the pace of change. It is very easy to characterise such people as 'capitalist roaders' when all they are doing is urging caution and moderation in 'building the socialist road'. In 1954/55 during the early 'co-operative construction' phase, Mao was accused of Left Opportunism when he advocated extremely rapid creation of mutual-aid teams and co-operatives. His break with the CCP in the mid-1920s was also as a result of his being criticised for Left Opportunism in organising the peasant uprising in Hunan and the Chingkangshan 'red bases'.

It is absurd to suppose that Liu Shaoqi wanted a return to 'capitalism' in the Western sense. It may be that he favoured a return to incentives on the Soviet model (and, indeed, that he wanted a rapprochement with the USSR) but that does not automatically mean he was a 'capitalist'. The propaganda does not and cannot convey such subtleties of meaning. Liu is a symbol of what the Cultural Revolution was against and as such it is convenient to vilify him as a 'capitalist roader'. It is a plot in the best melodramatic tradition of Chinese opera.

On the other hand, LOs are more complicated. Theoretically they cannot be 'to the left' of the Party, since the Party stands for a communist society and you can't get further left than that (so the theory goes). Where Mao and such LOs as the extreme Red Guards differ is in the pace of transformation from bourgeois revolution to socialism to communism. Left Opportunists are going too fast. They create unnecessary antagonisms among neutral groups such as the middle classes and thus stir up unnecessary trouble which may actually impede the very transformation for which they strive. That is why they are called reactionary and lumped together with the Right Opportunists.

The 'left' element may refer to people with 'unrealistic' ideas which may be characterised as 'utopianism'. This is a sneering term used by the 'pragmatic' consensus politicians of the CCP to denigrate people who wish to see Mao's, Marx's and Lenin's ideas of communism implemented immediately, and who reject the cautionary approach which preaches conciliation of groups antagonistic to the Party.

Left Opportunists cause more blind fury than Right Opportunists because: they claim, or are claimed, to be more radical than the Party. They can use the precedent of Mao's Left Opportunist lines in 1927, 1953-55, 1958-62 and 1966-67 to support their ideas;

They're saying what many Party members secretly believe to be morally correct.

By the way, if Lin Biao really was a Left Opportunist then the last place you would expect him to go would be the USSR, but where else could he go? If he was a Right Opportunist then he'd changed his mind since he led the assault on Liu Shaoqi.

Perhaps he thought the Cultural Revolution had gone far enough, had been scared off by the demonstration of the power of the 'organised masses'.

Perhaps it was merely a power struggle between him and Liu Shaoqi?

Perhaps Mao is senile?[53]

---

[53] He was, according to his doctor. He was also sadistic and entirely lacking in empathy. See: Zhisui Li, 1996. *The Private Life of Chairman Mao.* Arrow Books. ISBN 0 09 964881 4.

Perhaps the Russians had offered a deal to patch up the quarrel, in response to the overtures of the USA to China, which overtures Lin Biao could not have approved, had he really been a Left Opportunist.

The possibility of such a complicated scenario is strengthened by the reluctance of the CPR Government to make any comment at all on the incident [the death of Lin Biao].

Arcane and irrelevant?

That was what I scribbled on the plane home to London. The truth turned out to be less complicated: in their panicked departure after the assassination plot against Mao was discovered, Lin Biao, his wife Le Qun and their son Lin Liguo (the actual leader of the plot) didn't leave enough time for the pilot of their commandeered Trident jet to refuel before he was ordered at gunpoint to take off. That is why it ran out of fuel and crashed in Mongolia, killing all on board, before they could reach the USSR.

If these arguments about Left and Right Opportunists now seem arcane and irrelevant, that is a measure of the massive changes in China since the death of Mao in 1976, the 'reform' period that began in 1978, the vicious suppression of dissent in 1989, the explosive growth of gangster capitalism in the 1990s and the current reversion to stifling autocracy and the cult of personality. It is all desperately sad.

On the railroad home

We left Shanghai for Guangzhou the next morning, 22ⁿᵈ September, and for the following two days our train trundled through some of the loveliest countryside in China, famous for its chocolate box landscapes. Unfortunately I had run out of film so for that beautiful part of the Chinese journey I have to rely on memory, postcards and on the many coffee-table picture books that have been published since 1972.

On our last full day in China we visited Dongfang Commune (population about 50,000) where they grew rice and groundnuts in the Pearl River delta near Guangzhou. Our driver got lost in the countryside and we turned up unannounced at the wrong village – where we were nonetheless greeted like VIPs and everyone seemed very cheerful and relaxed, but I suspect the driver later paid dearly for his error. Although the China Travel Service itinerary did not go exactly to plan that day, we came away with a very favourable impression. There was perhaps a lesson for China Travel Service in this diversion: you don't have to plan everything to the last detail; it might have been useful to allow us to stray from the schedule a little more.

On 25ᵗʰ September we took the train to Shenzen, showed our passports and crossed the border. That evening we were on the plane to London.

It would take me a long time to digest and make sense of those very intense 26 days. As the reader who got this far will have noticed, I'm still trying to understand all I saw and heard, half a century later. This book has been an attempt to put the unforgettable into context.

I will probably never return to China. But I do wish its people (as distinct from its current government) long life, prosperity and the happiness they deserve.

The view of the Huangpu and the Bund woodland on the cover of the 1972 Shanghai guidebook.

Vladimir Ilyich Ulyanov exhorting the Shanghainese to work even harder. 18th September 1972. The slogan below reads, in part: 'The true Marxist-Leninist of all nations...' As we say in Scotland, 'Aye. Right.'

At last, a self-criticism with added contradictions

It is time for some self-criticism. Mao Zedong expected it of us all. Firstly, comrades will of course wish to examine the 'class origin' of the abject penitent kneeling before them. My grandparents were: a Shetland hand-knitter and housewife ('working class'?); a Clyde-trained shipwright from Lerwick ('red and expert comrade'?); an Essex tenant farmer's daughter ('rich peasant'?); and an uncertificated teacher of mathematics who came from a long line of plasterer's labourers in Tower Hamlets and had hauled himself up by his bootstraps, forsaking his plebeian origins ('bourgeois class enemy'?). Some 'bad elements' there without a doubt and my parents, while not wealthy, were both unashamedly middle class ('bourgeois class enemies') but, on the whole, it is not the worst of pedigrees. The really bad mark against me was having gained a university degree, albeit only because the State gave me a grant and paid my tuition fees, my parents being somewhat short of the readies in 1965-69. So, if we'd had a Cultural Revolution in Scotland I probably would have been 'sent up to the mountains and down to the countryside to learn from the peasants'. Only, as we shall see, I did that without being ordered to.

Like many of my 'baby boomer' generation born after the Second World War, I grew up in a social democratic country and was influenced by socialist ideas, particularly after I went to university. I read summaries of Marx, Engels and Stalin (not having the stamina to wade through the original tomes). I enjoyed inspiring if misleading tales of the Russian revolution in *Ten Days that Shook the World* by John Reed and *To the Finland Station* by Edmund Wilson, devoured Isaac Deutscher's unbalanced trilogy on Trotsky, and was inspired by Edgar Snow, Mao's hagiographer, who wrote *Red Star Over China* – a work that should really have been on the 'fiction' shelves of the university library.

Although I'd read Solzhenitsyn's *One Day in the Life of Ivan Denisovitch* back in 1962, when I was only 15, I somehow put that lesson to one side and managed to ignore the mounting evidence that Lenin, Trotsky, Stalin, Khrushchev, Mao Zedong, Zhou Enlai, Liu Shaoqi and Lin Biao were all, every one of them, accomplices in serial mass killings. In 1971 I even joined the Trotskyite International Socialists. I was expelled after three weeks, for 'right-wing deviationism', half an hour after I'd resigned in disgust and joined the Labour Party. I remained a Labour supporter for 35 years but after Blair's betrayals I settled for old-fashioned Scandinavian social democracy in the form of the Scottish National Party, the only outfit that tries seriously to protect the Welfare State, the National Health Service and the other socialist achievements of the 1945-51 Labour Government. There is a contradiction here, in that I may now appear to be intensely conservative. But what I and many others who have been on a similar political journey wish to conserve is the legacy of Clement Attlee and Nye Bevan, and to defend it against the ultra-rightist counter-revolutionaries spawned by Margaret Thatcher and still ruling the roost in Westminster.

Now we come to the Maoist principle of self-sufficiency that so inspired me and my contemporaries: Mao was not the first influential thinker to suggest that everyone who could should feed themselves from a vegetable garden. In England the idea goes back at least to the Diggers and Levellers of the 17th century and was popular in the 19th century when Charles Darwin tried it (on a private income) at his home in Kent. In the 1920s my aspirant bourgeois grandfather and his wealthier London friends went down to Dorset to help with the harvest every August, voluntarily. My own parents always grew vegetables in the 1950s when we lived in rural Oxfordshire and Warwickshire. The whole country had 'dug for victory' during the Second World War and in my childhood both Labour and Tory agriculture ministers had resolved that never again would Britain be dependent on vulnerable convoys of ships to feed us in wartime[54]. In Scotland the nation's 18th century hero Rabbie Burns was, famously, a self-reliant tenant farmer, albeit not a very successful agricultural role model; 19th century Edinburgh thinkers such as Patrick Geddes pioneered ideas about garden suburbs and promoted gardening in city centres; and from the 1920s to the 1950s local authorities in both Scotland and England built thousands of council houses with large back gardens, specifically to encourage tenants on low incomes to grow their own grub.

And then, around the year 1970, preceding the great climate crisis debate by 50 years, the Club of Rome, Greenpeace and other worthy NGOs had begun to warn us of the danger that we could make the planet uninhabitable for humans if we carried on polluting the air, the soil and the water. Those of us who took these warnings seriously began to think of alternative ways of making a living.

My generation had been influenced, subconsciously or not, by Maoist principles of horticultural self-sufficiency, even those of us who hadn't yet heard of Mao. Oddly enough, Mao knew remarkably little of agronomy or horticulture, subjects upon which he pontificated regularly and often with disastrous consequences. As soon as he was able, he'd run away from peasant labour and his tyrannical, violent father in the Hunan village of Shaoshan. Years later and far away from Hunan, his ignorant imperial edicts on deep ploughing, close planting and terracing would be followed slavishly in provinces where they often proved entirely unsuited to the terrain, soils, climate and crops. Showpiece communes such as Dai Zhai, supposedly exemplifying Mao's peasant wisdom, were in fact massively subsidised by the state for propaganda purposes and were far from self-sufficient.

I know all this now, from reading some of the many books about the horrific consequences of Maoism in China, all published long after the Scotland-China Association's 1972 study tour. What I regret (obviously in a spirit of Maoist self-criticism) is not observing more closely, from those train windows so long ago, what was actually happening in the countryside through which we passed so slowly. There were clues to be seen but I confess I didn't know how to look for them. And of course the Chinese Communist Party took us to model communes. We would have done the same. If the Scottish Tourist Board had been showing Chinese guests around Scotland in 1972, would it have bussed them to decaying mining villages like Shotts or pointed out the slums that still existed just off Edinburgh's Royal Mile? No, the guides would have shown them the beauties of Arthur's

---

[54] Despite this admirable principle, the UK currently imports about 80% of its food, mostly in foreign-owned ships (including Chinese vessels).

132

Seat, the Palace of Holyroodhouse and the view from the Castle Rock. The communes we saw were indeed inspiring but they were exceptional. We had all been 'taken in' to some extent, inspired by something that had been created through vast suffering and merciless oppression. I am ashamed of that but, paradoxically, I still find admirable the communes' inspiring principles of self-sufficiency.

When I left China I was much influenced by what Basil Davidson had called 'market gardening on a continental scale'. Gardening in China was acutely political. It was what the Cultural Revolution was all about, after all. Maoist zealots such as Jiang Qing (Madame Mao) alleged that it was 'bourgeois' to allow peasants to cultivate their own vegetable gardens and keep hens and pigs in addition to their duties to the collective. Selling their home-made lacework and knitwear for cash was even worse. It would lead to the restoration of capitalism, her 'Gang of Four' said. They were willing to assault, imprison, torture and even kill those who advocated the peasants' rights to private plots and the restoration of local markets for produce, livestock and handicrafts. Mao and his mouthpieces accused 'capitalist roaders' and 'right opportunists' such as Liu Shaoqi (and even Zhou Enlai) of wanting to overthrow the communes and collective endeavours altogether. After Mao's death, Deng Xiaoping and the 'capitalist roaders' won. Family-run gardens and local markets did rescue the Chinese economy from ruin after the Cultural Revolution. Resurgent capitalism would indeed follow in the 1980s and 1990s, when it was encouraged to go on the rampage in a state-controlled economy nearer to fascism than to social democracy. Throughout all this turmoil, China's endlessly patient and determined gardeners carried on planting every spring and harvesting every autumn, unless forcibly prevented from doing so.

Inspired partly by the people's communes, and partly by the Israeli kibbutz where my then wife had been a student volunteer, just eight months after I returned from China we started a crofting co-operative in a Shetland island with four friends we'd known as students. We shared accommodation in the two leaky old houses we were renovating; shared childcare; ate mostly communally; shared the work of creating productive gardens out of a derelict croft; and helped our elderly neighbours with harvest tasks and herding sheep in the common grazings. We each contributed what we could afford from our earnings in various part-time employments and we made no demands upon the State apart from medical care, statutory child allowances and of course the sheep subsidy that all crofters got. It was a social as well as a horticultural experiment. In some ways it looked like a commune but we never called it that. We certainly never had a revolutionary committee. Visitors who heard on the grapevine about our 'hippy commune' occasionally arrived off the ferry to see what was going on. Some of them helped with the work and received board, lodging, gratitude and lifelong friendship. Others just hung around smoking dope and philosophising until we were glad when they left. Our venture was, of course, entirely voluntary, unlike its Chinese counterparts. Like similar experiments in other parts of Scotland, it only lasted a few years until we went our separate ways and new opportunities beckoned elsewhere, but it didn't fail financially. The accounts book that I still have shows that it broke even. In modern parlance, it was 'sustainable'.

The legacy of our little experiment was threefold: the strapping toddlers grew into fine young people who in due course raised the best crop of all – our grandchildren; two derelict houses became habitable and remained so for many years; and some of us have been digging various gardens in every April of the fifty springs since then, trying to grow as much of our own food as we can. In a good year we might manage to produce by our 'diligent and frugal' labour a third to a half of what we eat, which is probably more than Mao's Da Zhai model commune did.

Mao Zedong, who had servants to prepare the finest delicacies for his meals and never did a stroke of physical work after 1949, would no doubt have urged comrades to 'struggle against' us as 'bourgeois romantic idealists'. It's a label I'm proud to wear. It beats being a serial killer.

Appendix: Harry Dickinson's report 'Rural China 1972'

Rural China 1972

by Harold Dickinson
School of Engineering Science
University of Edinburgh

A Report prepared for the
Commission on the Churches' Participation in Development
World Council of Churches, Geneva

Edinburgh
December 1972

RURAL CHINA, 1972

by

H. DICKINSON

School of Engineering Science
University of Edinburgh

SCHOOL OF ENGINEERING SCIENCE

(ELECTRICAL ENGINEERING)

UNIVERSITY OF EDINBURGH

RURAL CHINA, 1972

by

H. DICKINSON

School of Engineering Science
University of Edinburgh

A Report prepared for the :

Commission on the Churches' Participation in Development
World Council of Churches, Geneva.

Edinburgh,
December, 1972.

WEIGHTS AND MEASURES

Approximate conversions

Currency :

£1 = 5.5 yuan $1 = 2.3 yuan

1 yuan = £0.18 = $0.44

Weight :

1 catty (chin) = 0.5 kg = 1.1 lb

Area :

1 ha = 15 mow   1 acre = 6 mow

1 mow = $\frac{1}{15}$ ha = $\frac{1}{6}$ acre

I   INTRODUCTION

The prospect of visiting China to see that ultimate of collectivist development, the People's Commune, fascinates anyone interested in the problems and potentials of peasants in the poorer countries of the world. The visitor who, at best, can see only a small part of this new China is left bewildered by a society which takes in 700 million people, is both highly centralised and exhibits local autonomy, has solved by head-on collision the problem of land ownership, looks to social emulation and co-operation rather than to incentives and competition.

The explanation of this transformation is best sought by following the way in which the Chinese people came to accept the leadership of the Chinese Communist Party which gave them the will and the means to make the society we now see. The impetus for change is not exhausted and no one, including the Chinese themselves, has a clear idea of the future. There is no doubt that the wealth of China is increasing and that this wealth is much more uniformly distributed than in any other major nation of the world. In the richer agricultural areas many peasant families have accumulated and banked considerable amounts of purchasing power. The taste for consumer-goods is growing and shops, in both village and city, have large and varied stocks. Whether the social cohesion and unity of purpose so evident in the People's Communes will be maintained in the face of growing consumer expectations is a problem for the relatively near future.

The first stages in the establishment of co-operative production amongst the peasants of China has been described in the book "Socialist Upsurge in China's Countryside" edited in part by Mao Tse-Tung who wrote, in 1955, the following introductory comment to a section of this book :

- 1 -

Diligent and frugal operation ought to be the policy of all our agricultural co-operatives - of all our enterprises, in fact. Factories, stores, state owned and co-operative enterprises, all other enterprises - each should be run in keeping with the policy of diligence and frugality. This is a policy of economy, one of the basic policies of socialist economics.

China is a big country, but it is still very poor. We shall need a few score years before we can make China prosperous. Even then we still will have to be diligent and frugal. But it is in the coming few decades, during the present series of five-year plans, that we must particularly advocate diligence and frugality, that we must pay special attention to economy.

Many co-ops forget the need for economy. This is bad and should be corrected quickly. Co-ops which are run diligently and frugally can be found in every province, in every county. These should be publicized as examples for all to follow. Co-ops which are diligent and frugal, get high yields and are generally well-run, should be given awards. Those which are wasteful, obtain very low yields and are generally poorly run, should be criticised".

After a few years experience co-operatives gave way to People's Communes as vehicles for increasing agricultural production. As far as the individual field worker is concerned all improvements in agricultural technique have been summarized in the "Eight-point Charter for Agriculture" : - deep ploughing, irrigation projects, close planting, tool improvement, adequate manuring, good seed, plant protection and field management.

This present account is a brief view of China as it appears to an observer without previous experience of the country. It is an attempt to describe what was seen and heard in 26 days and it makes no pretence at predicting any future agricultural, or ideological developments in any part of the vast area of the People's Republic of China.

II ITINERARY IN CHINA

Entry to China is easier for organised parties than for individuals and the routes taken by visitors are thereby restricted to journeys between towns with adequate hotel accommodation. The travels described represent a compromise between the requests of a group (the Scotland-China Association), with substantial agricultural interests, and proposals for visits made by the China Travel Service. The request that all travel in China should be by train, so that conditions well away from urban areas could be seen, was met in full and several days were spent in travelling 5000 km by train.

Details of each day's activities are given in chronological order :-

30 August : Arrived at Hong Kong after flight from London.

31 August : Left Kowloon by train for border station. Crossed International Bridge to Sumchun border station in the People's Republic. Met by interpreters and went to Canton by train.

1 September : Da Li People's Commune. Saw wide range of agricultural and ancilliary activities including machine fabrication and repair shop, pig farm, grain mill, health centre, herbal pharmacy and crop-irrigation pumps. Had discussions with members of the Commune Revolutionary (Management) Committee. Interviewed peasants in their homes. Commune produce lunch.

2 September : Chungshan Medical College and Canton No.I and No.2 Hospitals. Saw outpatient, cardiac, orthopaedic and maternity departments. Discussion with patients who had had severed limbs re-attached. Long discussion with members of Medical College Revolutionary Committee.

3 September : Peoples Park, site of a massacre in 1927, Museum of Archaeology, and Institute of Peasant Studies where Mao Tse-tung instructed 300 cadres in 1926. Left Canton by train for Chengchow.

4 September : Travelled by train through Hunan, Hupeh and Honan provinces. Crossed River Yangtze by Wuhan Bridge. Saw effect of severe drought in areas with and without adequate irrigation.
Arrived Chengchow in the evening and saw "The Red Lantern", a revolutionary opera.

5 September : Arts and crafts factory, producing jade ornaments for export, and a textile factory producing cloth from cotton and synthetic fibres. Discussions with Revolutionary Committees in both factories.

6 September : Irrigation station nearing completion on south bank of Hwang Ho (Yellow River), a Fruit-tree Research Institute and Chengchow Fruit Farm. Discussed problems of the use of chemical pesticides and biological controls with Research Institute Revolutionary Committee and later inspected apple crop, on Fruit Farm, with varieties developed by the Research Institute. Left Chengchow on night train for Peking.

7 September : Arrived Peking and later visited the Sino-Cuban Friendship People's Commune which specialises in production of fruit, pigs, ducks and horticultural products for the Peking market. Interviewed 'Barefoot Doctor' and peasant families.

8 September : Day long bus trip to Great Wall and Ming Tombs. Saw evening performance of "The White-haired Girl", a revolutionary ballet.

9 September : Day long visit to Pei Tah (Peking) University.

10 September : Tour of Peking including Forbidden City and Summer Palace. Left by train for Nanking.

11 September : Travelled by train through Shantung and Anwei provinces. Arrived at Nanking. Visited the bridge over the Yangtze River and Sun Yat Sen Mausoleum.

12 September : Drum Tower Hospital, to see operations performed under acupuncture anaesthesia. Primary School.

13 September : Junior Middle School, to observe tuition and practical instruction in workshops and school garden. Inspected small factory making mercury switches.

14 September : Travelled by train from Nanking to Wusih. Visited a small factory, making plaster statuettes.

15 September : Factory making ferro-concrete boats. Discussed technical, organisational problems with members of the Revolutionary Committee, sailed on canal in boats built by the factory. Ho La People's Commune to see fish pond management, pearl culturing, silk-worm rearing and side-line industries. Discussed commune organisation and the use of pesticides and fertilisers with members of the Revolutionary Committee. Saw performance of "The Red Detachment of Women", a revolutionary opera.

16 September :   Silk-reeling factory to see all stages of silk thread production from cocoon to bundled yarn. Discussed factory organisation with Revolutionary Committee and had long interview with Chairman of the Committee.

17 September :   Travelled by train from Wusih to Shanghai.

18 September :   Housing estate and saw associated primary school, housewives light-bulb factory, primary school and old peoples reading room. Spent afternoon recording retail prices in shops in a principal shopping street.

19 September :   "July 1st" People's Commune in suburbs of greater Shanghai. Saw rice fields, irrigation, a dairy farm, a pig farm, chicken and geese rearing, mushroom growing, workshops for repairing and fabricating farm equipment, furniture workshop and an electric motor assembly plant.

20 September :   Had discussions with members of Fudan University and later visited turbo-generator factory. Saw performance of the Shanghai Acrobat Troupe.

21 September :   Shanghai Industrial Exhibition. Entertained by school children in "Children's Palace".

22 September :   Travelled by train through Chekiang and Kiangsi provinces.

23 September :   Continued train journey, through Hunan and Kwangtung provinces, to Canton.

24 September :   Village in Tung Fang Commune in Sikiang (Pearl River) delta. Saw private plots, irrigation works, farm machinery and use of pesticides. Interviewed peasant families.

25 September :   Left Canton by train for Shumchun. Crossed International Bridge and took train to Kowloon. Left Hong Kong by air for London.

III GEOGRAPHICAL OUTLINE AND CLIMATE

The People's Republic of China, which has a superficial area of some $9.6 \times 10^6 \ km^2$, lies between longitude 73° East, on the Western frontier with Tadjikstan, and 135° East on the North-eastern border of the Ussuri River; and between 53° North on the Northern border of the Amur River and 20° North on the South China Sea. The Southern limit is extended to 17° North by Hainan Island.

With the exception of the highly fertile Red Basin of Szechuan, on the upper reaches of the Yangtse River, the most populous areas occur in that third of China to the east of a line from the Vietnam border to Peking. This Eastern zone, Inner or Agricultural China, is the area where traditional Chinese agriculture has flourished for centuries and includes the Lower and Middle Yangtse Plains, the North China Plain and the North-East Plain. These plain lands cover about 1×10^6 km^2, stand between sea level and 500 m, have relatively high rainfall and are watered by the great rivers. The coastal provinces of the East have low gently sloping hills, rising to 500 m, and are important areas for fruit growing.

The mountain ranges and basins of North and North-West China take in much of the Gobi desert and extend over another third of the country. This is a region of low rainfall, poor soils quite unsuitable for Chinese traditional agriculture and, apart from a few favoured basins, supports a low density population of nomadic or semi-nomadic peoples.

The remaining third of China, supporting only a sparse population, is the high Tibetan plateau. Here there are poor soils, low rainfall, a frost free summer of less than two months in the year, and considerable areas above 4000 m with permanent frost.

The main agriculturally productive areas of Inner China are in the sub-tropical zone shading Northward into the temperate zone and Southward into the tropical zone along the Southern coast and on Hainan Island. Most rainfall occurs during May to October and takes the form of monsoons, from the Pacific Ocean, the China Sea and the Indian Ocean, which pass to the North and West becoming dryer the further they penetrate inland. Rainfall of 750 mm per annum occurs in the South-East, 500 mm per annum in the plains of the North and less than 250 mm per annum in the far North and West. The major rivers, crossing the country from West to East, have a long history of flooding following very heavy rainfall but the dangers of flooding have been much reduced by irrigation, drainage, hydro-power and flood-control works.

As a consequence of these great climatic variations Chinese agriculturalists are able to raise, on a large scale, all the major crops of the temperate and sub-tropical parts of the world. Northern agriculture is characterised by the growing of wheat and millet as staple crops together with soya and cotton. In Southern agriculture rice is the staple, much tea is cultivated and bamboo grows freely. The Southern coastal fringe of the mainland and Hainan Island produce a wide range of tropical products.

The visit to China described in this report was restricted to the Canton-Peking-Shanghai-Canton triangle - the area that supports most of the Chinese people and includes the alluvial lands bordering the Hwang Ho (Yellow River), the Yangtse, and the Sikiang (Pearl River).

IV LAND USE AND POPULATION DISTRIBUTION

China is a country where agriculture and related activities are undertaken by 80% of the population of more than 760×10^6 people. About 10% of the population is engaged in manufacturing industry which grows steadily on a base of indigenous mineral wealth and power potential; these enable the People's Republic to be economically independent of the outside world. The distribution of industry, a legacy of pre-liberation days, is restricted to areas about and to the North-east of Peking and around Shanghai. The implementation of current industrialisation plans is leading to the spread of producer's goods industries throughout the country.

Intensive agriculture, on modified traditional lines, within the inner (Eastern) third of China remains the base of China's existence. The total area of China is $9.6 \times 10^6 \text{ km}^2$ and, taking the population as 760×10^6 persons, the average density of inhabitants is 80 per km^2. In the more agriculturally productive areas densities of over 200 per km^2 occur. The population natural growth rate is usually given as 1.8% to 2.4% per annum but, with extensive family limitation propaganda campaigns, there are indications that this rate may have been reduced to 1.4%. This reduced figure still represents a population doubling time of 50 years. In many ways China is managing to provide for its growing population and signs of over population are not seen in even the most densely populated areas. Nevertheless dealing with an increase of population in excess of 8×10^6 per annum puts great strains on the country's social and economic systems. The production of staple grain crops is keeping pace with population growth but considerable demands are put on the most productive areas of Inner China - the black and brown soils of the Northern plains and the heavy rice soils of the Lower Yangtse and Szechuan.

The main elements of land use in China may be roughly summarised :-

Total Land Area	$9.6 \times 10^6 \text{ km}^2$	(100%)
*Deserts/Wastelands	$3.7 \times 10^6 \text{ km}^2$	(40%)
Pastures/Rough Grazing	$2.7 \times 10^6 \text{ km}^2$	(28%)
Agriculturally Productive	$1.1 \times 10^6 \text{ km}^2$	(11%)
Potentially Cultivable	$1.1 \times 10^6 \text{ km}^2$	(11%)
*Forests/Woodlands	$1.0 \times 10^6 \text{ km}^2$	(10%)

(*As a result of intensive afforestation in desert margins and wastelands another $1.0 \times 10^6 \text{ km}^2$ of young trees are believed to have been planted in the last decade).

Within the agriculturally productive land area some 90% is used for cropping; roads, housing, buildings and other works amount to, perhaps, 7% or 8%. The balance is made up by wood growing areas, including tree linings to roads and canals, and graves. Traditionally Chinese graves have been spread widely over agricultural land rather than in concentrated burial grounds. With changing fashions and beliefs burial has given way to cremation. Burials still occurring are made at depths of 3 m or more in agricultural land which is then reinstated. Many traditional burial sites have been covered in the same way.

V   FROM LANDLORD TO PEOPLES COMMUNE

1. Traditional China : Cultivation in China has a
very long history during which time redistribution, division
and sub-division under successive rulers produced a society
in which almost all the fertile land was owned by landlords,
large and small, many of them absentees. The land was occupied
by peasant proprietors or, more numerously, by tenants with
family plots, of perhaps 0.25 ha, in several separated
fragments. Rents paid by tenants were largely in kind. 50%
of total production was a common figure but rents of 75% or
even 90% were paid. In such a situation efficient agriculture
and flood control in the fertile river basins were both
impossible. Yields were low and even in good years only bare
subsistence was possible. In the all too frequent bad years
millions starved or fled to other equally impoverished areas.
Yet, despite all this deprivation, the population grew.

Little changed for the peasant as a result of the
Revolution of 1911 in which Sun Yat-sen and the Kuomintang
overthrew the Empire and promised "equalisation of rights in
the land". There was further disruption during the war years
from the Japanese invasion of Manchuria in 1931 to their
final collapse in 1945. A further four years of civil war
led to the establishment of the Peoples Republic in 1949 under
the leadership of the Chinese Communist Party and its
Chairman, Mao Tse-tung.

2. Land Redistribution (1949 to 1952) : After the
establishment of the Peoples Republic the redistribution of
land continued according to the pattern established in the
Communist controlled areas in the late 1930's and throughout
the war years. Titles to land were taken from the landlord
class and transferred to the peasant cultivators. Some of the
larger estates were retained by the new state as State Farms
occupying a little more than 5% of the land; the peasants there
became wage earners. This redistribution was of the greatest
social significance and when completed, by 1952, the benefits
of a stable system where the peasant has full security of
tenure of the land he cultivates had largely been achieved.
Further increase in agricultural production continued to be
limited by the small size of individual holdings which were

too small to support adequate irrigation and drainage works
and to take advantage of scientific farming and land management.

3. Collectivisation and Co-operatives (1952 to 1957) :
The collectivisation of agricultural production was achieved
in a number of stages. At first, and without any change in
ownership of land, tools or stock, small groups of peasant
cultivators shared their tools and the tasks of cultivation,
ran stock in common and were able to adopt better crop
rotation and land use. These mutual aid teams grew into the
"Semi-Socialist Co-operatives" in which groups of some 20 or
30 households, with perhaps 150 persons, carried out mutual
aid in a more integrated fashion. Further advantages of
increased size and specialised division of labour were soon
attained, but these groups were not large enough to deal with
major works of land improvement. Larger units were organised
and 740,000 "Advanced Socialist Co-operatives", of 100
households or more, were set up by the end of 1957. Once more
the limits of size and organisation soon became apparent and
in the "The Great Leap Forward" of 1958 the counties, the old
basic administrative units, were changed in to executive bodies
concerned with planning and production when the advanced
co-operatives were regrouped into 26,000 "People's Communes".

4. "Peoples Communes" (1958 onwards) : The 26,000
Communes were able to command large labour forces and to
undertake wide ranging programmes of water conservation,
including drainage, irrigation and terracing, land use
rationalisation, use of fertilisers, improvement of crops, and
to begin social improvements. Many Communes were found to be
over large and unweildly and after some sub-division 78,000
separate People's Communes were established. These 78,000
Communes are joined to the central government though 2000
counties in 22 provinces. There are also some state farms and
some large farms run by the People's Liberation Army which
account for about 7% of agriculturally productive land.

Since the "Great Proletarian Cultural Revolution" which
began in 1965, the management of each commune is a
Revolutionary Committee in which there is "three-in-one"
representation of Cadres, including Communist Party

Representatives, People's Militia, a reserve force of able-bodied men and women, and the peasant masses. Under each Commune there are between 5 and 25 Production Brigades which are sub-divided into between 5 and 20 Production Teams. Each Brigade and Team has its own "three-in-one" Revolutionary Committee. Table 1, below, indicates the structure of a number of Communes, Brigades and Production Teams.

The population of a Commune depends on local agricultural conditions, population density and the historical settlement pattern. Natural villages are the bases of Brigades or Production Teams. Production Teams may include 30 to 100 households, Brigades 100 to 1000 and Communes 2000 to 20000. The population of individual Communes ranges from 6000 to over 60000 persons. The area of individual Communes is also very variable, depending on land quality and local communications, and may be as small as 1000 ha or as large as 20000 ha. The Communes of smaller area are likely to be intensively cultivated; the larger only partly cultivated with, perhaps, two-thirds or more of the area given over to rough grazing or forestry.

People's Communes show a considerable degree of autonomy in their day to day operation and the greatest emphasis is put on self-help and self-reliance. Their connection with the Chinese State, through County and Provincial Authorities, is principally concerned with the planning of production, the collection and distribution of surplus agricultural production, taxation, and the supply of artificial fertilisers. All agricultural production in China is related to a national plan in which grain and protein production is uppermost. After assessment of past performance and mutual consultation each organisation, be it Province, County, Commune, Brigade or Team, receives a target which it tries to over-fulfill. It is the duty of the Party Members, who play leading roles in all Revolutionary Committees to ensure that the peasant masses are properly consulted and infused with enough enthusiasm to ensure that all reasonable efforts are made to pass the production targets. To this end all important policies and principal work measures are adopted by the collective leadership of the Party Committee and the decisions of the Party Committee are carried out by the Revolutionary Committee

TABLE I : STRUCUTRE OF SOME COMMUNES

	Principal Crops etc	Number of Persons	Number of Households	Area under cultivation (ha)	Members of Revolutionary Committee	Number of Brigades	Number of Production Teams
COMMUNE							
Sino-Cuban (Peking)	Wheat, Pigs, Ducks	38000		3600	40	6	59
Ho La (Wusih)	Grain, Fish	14820	4080	1060	21	7	81
"July 1st" (Shanghai)	Vegetables, Grain	16836	4122		19	11	88
Hongquiao (Shanghai)	Vegetables, Rice	26700		13000			
Da Li (Canton)	Rice, Pigs	63000	19000	~~17000~~ 4000		19	237
Huadong (Canton)	Rice, Pigs	56500		4800		24	365
Tung Fang (Canton)	Rice, Ground-nut	50000+	12000		39	25	352
BRIGADE							
In Ho La Commune	Fish, Silk	3962	986	178	9	-	18
In Tachai Commune (Shansi)	Grain	438		53			
PRODUCTION TEAMS							
In Tung Fang Commune	Rice	404	72	53			-
In Chengkuan Commune (Chekiang)	Grain, Silk	253	55	27			-

of the Commune. After the basic foodstuff needs of the Commune members are satisfied all surpluses are sold to the State through local purchasing agencies. The revenue from such sales accrues to Commune funds. Taxation represents 5 to 7% of production as assessed some years ago and with productivity increases it now accounts for much less, perhaps only 2 or 3% of gross production. The tax requirement is subject to review at 5 yearly intervals but it is not seen as a burden on production.

Commune funds have to pay for all fixed capital inputs to the production process, such as tools, machines, irrigation or drainage works, and for artificial fertilisers. In addition a wide range of social services, medical, educational, and welfare, are paid for from the same funds. After all payments have been made the balance is distributed in cash or kind to the Commune members. Examples of annual expenditure accounting are :-

<u>Da Li Commune, Canton</u> :

Year : 1971 - similar result expected for 1972

<u>Gross Income</u>	14×10^6 yuan ($\pounds 6.1 \times 10^6$) : (100%)			
Expenditure	Production costs	: 28% of gross income		
	Accumulation for investment:	8% "	"	"
	Public welfare and education	: 3.5%"	"	"
	State taxes	: 1.5%"	"	"
	Distributed as personal income	: 59% "	"	"
<u>Food grain production</u>	32×10^6 kg	: (100%)		
<u>Sold to State, including tax</u>	9×10^6 kg (approx)	: (28%)		
<u>Distributed to Commune Members</u>	23×10^6 kg (approx)	: (72%)		

Chiaoli Production Team, Chengkuan Commune, Chekiang :-

Year : 1971

Gross income : 87978 yuan (₤38000)   (100%)

Expenditure : Production costs   :21427 yuan   (24.4%)
               Accumulation for investment :13068   "   (14.7%)
               State taxes   : 3386   "   (3.9%)
               Distributed as personal   :50097   "   (57.0%)
               income

Food grain   :288530 kg   (100%)
production

Sold to State,   :126595 kg   (44%)
including tax

Distributed to   :101100 kg   (35%) ⎫
Commune nembers   ⎬ (56%)
Team reserves   :60835 kg   (21%) ⎭

Just as the primary aim is agricultural self-sufficiency,
self-reliance is the second important feature of all Communes.
In addition to land irrigation, crop improvements and the
introduction of animal husbandry, self-sufficiency covers
the making of clothing, shoes, tools, ropes, baskets and
other items that are in constant use in the life of the
Commune. In particular all Communes have workshops where
tools and simple machines, such as hand-operated winnowers,
huskers, and rice-transplanters, can be fabricated or repaired.
These workshops have a variety of simple machine tools as
well as carpenter's and blacksmith's shops and may employ from
30 to over 100 workers. As the Communes have become more
efficient and productivity has increased the demand for
agricultural labour has lessened and more effort has been
put into non-agricultural production units. Using locally
available raw materials many Communes produce artificial
fertilisers and pesticides as well as having teams engaged
in brick making and the construction of houses and farm
buildings. Some Communes now produce all the furniture
necessary for their own needs and sell part of their production
outwith the Commune. The most advanced Communes have complete
factories for quite complex products such as small electric
motors. All these activities add to the Commune revenue and

non-agricultural income may account for 25% of gross income.

The Commune members receive their income partly in cash and partly in kind, including a substantial amount of grain (up to 1 kg per head per day). In addition each member of the Commune has a private plot of 0.07 mow (47 m^2), combined to give family holdings, on which vegetables are grown for human consumption or for feeding one or more privately owned pigs as well as chickens and ducks. Most families are self-sufficient for eggs and vegetables and any surplus may be sold to augment the cash income of the family.

5. Communes + Electrification (1965 to 1980?) : The evolution of the People's Commune has enabled the Chinese people, within a period of 20 years, to come to terms with their environment to the extent of being regularly and adequately fed in a remarkably egalitarian society that provides basic medical, welfare and educational services. This social revolution has been achieved by the planning capacity of the Communist Party of China and the dedicated hard work of the Chinese people. Diligence and frugality provided the capital for the irrigation and drainage schemes that have led to stable and reliable agriculture practices and to increased productivity of the land. After the completion of this stage of development a new social revolution is coming to the Chinese countryside in which simple mechanisation and the widespread provision of rural electricity supplies are reducing, for the first time, the back-breaking labour of the peasant cultivator. Small, 9 h.p., walking-tractors and larger, 35 h.p. and 45 h.p., four-wheel tractors are being introduced to agriculture. Trucks, buses and jeeps are replacing hand-carts and horse drawn carts. Rice transplanters are beginning to be effective. The greatest social impact of all the technological innovations has been made by electricity which is already supplied to, perhaps, half of the Communes in the Eastern agricultural parts of China. Now electrically power water-pumps have taken over from manual pumps for lifting water in many irrigation systems. Large pumps are used on the main channels and canals and small pumps of 3 or 4 h.p. are now standard equipment in many Communes. In all these

ways labour has been made available for new agricultural
and non-agricultural activities. With the availability of
electricity it has been relatively easy to set up powered
plant for the processing of agricultural products and for
other Commune manufacturing industries. There are plans
for all Communes to have electricity and to have some
measure of mechanisation by 1980.

In travelling through rural China by railway the contrast
between Communes with electricity and those without is most
marked when the intensity of labour and the superficial
aspects of prosperity are compared.

VI   THE BASES OF AGRICULTURAL PRODUCTION

The "Eight-point Charter for Agriculture" has already
been mentioned. All the points are important in achieving
reliable and high agricultural yields. In practice some
order of priority has had to be established and in most of the
areas visited the existence of such priorities was evident.
The greatest emphasis has been put on irrigation and drainage
works, large and small, to solve both agricultural production
and social problems in a country where flood and drought
alternated. Agricultural production has been increased by
continuing, more intensively, the high density planting of
grain crops, by introducing some chemical fertilizers and a
variety of plant protection measures, by introducing new plant
strains and varieties to suit the various regions of the
country, and by starting a programme of mechanisation and
electrification.

1. Irrigation and Drainage : In China the term water
conservation is used to describe a wide range of activities
from major river control and large scale afforestation to the
smaller projects carried out by Communes or Production Teams.
In the past tree felling and overgrazing of pastureland in
the middle and upper reaches of the rivers led to extensive
erosion of fertile soils and to large quantities of silt
being carried by the major rivers, especially the Hwang Ho
(Yellow River) which owes its name to the appearance of the
suspended solids it carries. The average silt content of the

Hwang Ho, in its middle reaches near Chengchow, is 8.8 kg/m^3 with a maximum of 33 kg/m^3. Over the centuries canals have been dug and many raised river embankments have been created by dredging the settled silt from river beds. Despite such measures flooding was never controlled fully and in periods of neglect rivers broke through and overwhelmed the plains. Occasionally these rivers changed their courses following extensive flooding. On coming to power the Chinese Communist Party stressed the need to control the great rivers. Major flood control schemes were started on a number of rivers including the Hwang Ho, Yangtse, Huai and Haiho. On the upper reaches terracing and afforestation schemes were undertaken to control run-off and to reduce erosion and silting. Lower down, at the exits of the great gorges through the mountains, high dams have been constructed to form water storage and electrical power production reservoirs. At the Liuchia and Sanmen Gorges, there are electrical generation capacities of over 1000 MW on the Hwang Ho. On the lower reaches of the rivers low-head dams retain water for irrigation as well as for flow and flood control. Silt that settles in the reservoirs and on the river beds is extracted and spread over nearby agricultural land.

Water stored in the reservoirs can be released to maintain adequate river water for extractive pumping stations, or be fed to gravity flow canals. In both ways water is supplied to irrigate large agricultural areas. Extractive stations have electrically driven pumps and a large scheme may take 60 m^3/sec and raise water 30 or even 100 m. In a project near Chengchow electric motors of 380 kW were lifting water to 86 m in two stages. It is taken as a working rule that 1000 ha of agricultural land has an irrigation requirement of 1 to 1.5 m^3/sec of water.

In providing water from the large State or Provincial schemes no charge is made to the Communes that benefit. Similarly no charge is made for the electric power used. Water conservation and electrical power supply are state services that provide essential inputs for both agriculture and industry.

At Commune or Production Team level all irrigation and
drainage works are carried out by Commune or Team members.
Any pumps or other equipment that cannot be made within the
Commune have to be purchased from the State with Commune
funds.

Both large scale projects and those on the Communes
are carried out on a labour-intensive basis with very many
labourers working at one time. 100000 workers may be organised
to carry materials for a dam, or other major earthwork, at
slack times for agricultural work. The achievements since
liberation can be illustrated by the growth of the area of
irrigated land. In 1949 some 20×10^6 ha was inherited by
the People's Republic, by 1959 this has been increased by
more than 40×10^6 ha and the effort to irrigate more land
continues.

2. <u>Intensive High-Density Planting</u> : The Chinese
tradition of rice cultivation is a high seed rate, close
spacings, high plant population and heavy fertilization. To
maintain high densities and to cut the time that the crop
occupies the land transplanting is widely practiced. Much
effort is now directed toward developing an effective hand-
powered rice transplanter. Much labour is expended on hand
weeding and thinning so that it is difficult to find any other
plant species in a paddy field. Wheat production is carried
out at similar intensity. The preferred rotation is a three
crop cycle : rice 75 days; rice 90 days; wheat 105 days.

3. <u>Fertilizers</u> : Chinese cultivators use organic
fertilizers in the largest quantities obtainable. A number
of artificial fertilizers and mineral additives are in
common use with an emphasis on those that may be made in
small, Commune or Production Team, factories rather than in
large centralised manufacturing plant.

The most frequently used fertilizers are :

(a) <u>Human Waste</u>

Chinese agriculture is well known to be based on the
widespread use of untreated faeces and urine. This remains
the principal source of plant nutrients. In the past middens

adjacent to dwellings, and accessible to roaming pigs, were a serious health hazard as a source of fly-borne disease and intestinal worms, especially tapeworms. One of the first dicta of Chairman Mao was to encourage the removal of all middens from the vicinity of houses. At the present time this waste material is collected daily, from latrines and bucket lavatories, and stored in concrete tanks. After dilution with water, this liquid manure is carried in buckets and applied close to the plants by long-handled scoops or ladles.

(b) Farm Yard Manure

The droppings of pigs, cattle, water buffaloes, and horses are collected and rotted down in pits or concrete tanks before use. Large scale pig production units are an important source of manure and this importance will increase when the target, set by Mao Tse-tung, of one pig per person in the whole of China is attained. In many Communes all animal manure is collected as part of the effort to ensure self-sufficiency in grains; in others part of this organic material is retained by the peasants for use on their private plots.

(c) Compost, Green Manure and Silt

All materials that may be composted are collected assiduously with the exception of rice straw which is used largely as fuel for cooking. The leaves of trees, lotus, soya and all other vegetable wastes are composted together with river mud, if available, and the compost is used to enrich land before planting. Green beans are grown and dug in before planting cotton and between wheat crops. Clovers are grown within the grain production rotations. Weeds and silt dredged from fish-ponds are used as a highly nutritive fertilizer, especially for mulberry trees.

(d) Wood Ash

Any wood waste, materials too fibrous to compost and rice straw are used as fuel for cooking and boiling pig food. The resulting ash is used on private plots.

(e) <u>Artificial Fertilizers</u>

Chemical fertilizers are widely used as additives to the manures and composts; most Communes visited used between 10 and 30%. The purchase of artificials from the state is one of the major items of expenditure of the Commune and every effort is made to minimise their use. To support self-sufficiency, and to reduce demands on available transport, small local fertilizer producing factories are widespread in China. The preferred method of Nitrogen fixation is to produce ammonia from coal or gas. Ammonia, in a 20% solution, is applied by hand direct to the growing crops. This is much the most common fertilizer used in China. Crushed limestone and treated crushed phosphatic rocks appeared to be generally available and other materials mentioned included calcium phosphate, ammonium phosphate, ammonium sulphate, a Nitrogen fertilizer to increase boll size in cotton, and ammonium carbonate was said to be used on poor soils.

4. Plant Protection : Every effort is made to use crop hygiene procedures, to prevent plant diseases spreading, such as ensuring that no host plants are left for over-wintering invertebrate pests. A number of insecticides and fungicides are in general use as sprays or dusts. The most usual form of application being by back-pack pressurised sprays or lever-operated sprays and dusters. The use of 223 (D.D.T.) and 666 (Benzene hexachloride) is widespread, and much grain production is dependent on such general insecticides. On one Commune 666 was sprayed on to fish ponds to kill surface insects and water beetles that attack fish. A compound, known as 1605, was used to spray rice on another Commune where great care was taken to protect the operatives from contact with the spray; after spraying red triangular 'skull and crossbones' flags were erected at field corners to ensure that no one brushed against the newly sprayed crop. There is concern in some Communes about possible dangers to poultry, farm stock and humans from the cumulative effects of such pesticides, and the need to find pest-specific biological controls was mention on several occasions. The Fruit Tree Research Institute at Chengchow was particularly concerned with this general problem.

However the only biological control encountered was on a
Commune near Shanghai where a culture from a research
institute was grown, on an enriched protein jelly, by children
in a middle school. The culture is called "Spring Thunder"
and is used to control a disease that produced brown spots
on paddy leaves.

In travelling through China large numbers of insect
attracting lamps were seen in the fields in areas with
electricity supplies. The lamps are vertically mounted
fluorescent or discharge tubes giving a very blue light.
The top of each lamp fitting is protected from rain by a small
roof of straw thatch and a container below the lamp (oil-
filled?) traps the attracted insects. The lamps are mounted
just above the level of the top of the crop and in some areas
there are arrays of such lamps with separations of 200 or
300 m.

All plant protective chemicals and equipment seen had
been made in China.

In a number of special eradication campaigns vast
numbers of people have all but eliminated mosquitoes, flies,
rats and sparrows. It is quite remarkable to see farms with
hundreds of pigs and to find no more than 5 or 6 flies.
The well known 'gong-beating' campaign against sparrows was
effective but the populations of many other bird species
were also decimated. As a result of this and of the very
intensive use of land, which leaves few nesting sites,
Chinese agricultural areas appear to be almost birdless.
However, in the Nanking-Wusih area autumn flocks of several
thousand sparrows are to be seen in the grainfields.

5. Variety selection : A number of institutes are
developing varieties of grains and fruits to meet regional
requirements. Selection is also carried out by specialist
groups on Communes which collect a number of, say, rice strains
from other communes and conduct field trials to find the best
strain for local conditions. Such trials are largely
empirical as few Communes would have any members trained in
genetics. The research and development institutes do their
own field trials on Communes and pass some theoretical

knowledge to selected Commune members with adequate Middle
or High School education.

6. Mechanisation : Chinese agriculture remains highly
labour intensive. The use of draught animals is widespread
and, on some Communes, there are farms and breeding stations
for water buffaloes, horses, donkeys, mules and oxen.
Manpower is still used widely for moving heavy loads by
barrows, carts and shoulder pole baskets.

There are a number of mechanical devices which have a
long history of use in China and can still be seen in many
places. These include 'persian' wheels for water raising, and
'dragon's-spine' water pumps driven by hand-levers, pedals or
treadmills. Large stone rollers, in the form of truncated
cones, drawn by animals are commonly used for threshing. Stone
flour mills of several different types are still in use.
Other simple mechanical aids, seen on all Communes, are hand-
or treddle-powered threshing, winnowing and husking machines.
The designs of many of these machines were widely distributed
as self-help pamphlets and have been the basis for a low-
cost first stage on the road to mechanise agriculture. At
that time, most state capital was devoted to heavy industry
and power production in the Stalinist, development by
industrialisation, phase of the Chinese Revolution. With
the later change to an idigenous development model,
agriculture became the key activity supported by ancilliarv
light industries and backed by heavy industry.

Now mechanisation in agriculture is proceeding rapidly
with priority given to lighten the heavier work done by
Commune members, especially water pumping and carrying,
deep ploughing and land preparation. Threshing and winnowing
machines are being changed from manual to powered operation
at a slower rate. Sowing, hoeing, weeding, transplanting
and harvesting remain largely manual operations as do cotton
and fruit picking. Irrigation, including small scale
operations, is in rapid change with traditional man-powered
pumps being replaced by electrical, diesel or gasoline
pumps.

The motive power for much of Chinese mechanisation of agriculture is the 9 h.p., water-cooled, diesel, walking-tractor (a single-axle tractor), which is used to cultivate the less heavy soils, to haul trailers and to drive compressor motors for crop spraying, water pumping and grain milling. This tractor is built in China in large numbers and is seen everywhere. There are lesser numbers of four wheeled tractors with drivers' cabs. One type, of 35 h.p., seen was of Czech origin, and a more modern, 45 h.p. model, had been manufactured in China at the Shanghai Tractor Factory.

Most of the 78000 Communes and the 3000 State Farms have workshops making hand tools and the simpler machines as well as maintaining and repairing almost all the mechanical and electrical equipment that is in use.

Mechanisation is backed by the Chinese Ministry for Agricultural Engineering, (separate from the Ministry for Agriculture) which has some 30 provincial and regional research institutes. In addition most Communes have a small group of skilled workers who modify and adapt existing machines and who are making great efforts to produce satisfactory hand-powered rice transplanters.

An average Commune may be expected to have 20 or 30 tractors, 20 trucks and jeeps, several horse drawn carts and tractor trailers and 20 or more electric pumps. During a visit to Ho La Commune a Production Brigade, with a population of 3962, producing rice, fish and silkworms, listed the equipment made outside the Commune as 11 walking tractors, 14 threshing machines, 13 water pumps, 3 powered vessels of 50 tons and 79 small boats, mostly concrete. The San Tsun Production Team, part of a poor Commune near Canton, is based on a population of 404 and has a few items of powered equipment : one tractor, two sets of electrically pumped irrigation sprayers, an electric threshing machine and an electric mill for grinding grain for human consumption. Nine oxen and 8 water buffaloes are used for ploughing. The prices paid by this Production Team for powered equipment and draught animals are :-

```
Electric Threshing Machine  :   200 yuan (£90)
Electric Irrigation Pump    :   280 yuan (£120)
Walking Tractor             :  1500 yuan (£650)
Ploughing Water Buffalo     :   600 yuan (£260)
```

7. **Electrification** : China has a large hydro-power
potential as well as large coal reserves. An electric power
programme has led to the establishment of a large number
of small, up to 2 MW, hydro-electric stations with others as
large as 1000 MW. A widespread high-voltage network
distributes this power throughout the populated areas.
All the Communes visited had electricity and distribution poles
were seen throughout most of the railway journeys in China.
In the Communes the electricity supply is standard 220/380 V,
3-phase, 50 Hz. Water pumping, by electric pumps ranging
from 3 or 4 kW to over 400 kW, is an important feature of
Chinese agriculture and wherever electricity is supplied
manual and diesel-powered pumps are supplanted by electric
pumps. The availability of electricity and small 3-phase
induction motors enables the simple conversion of hand
operated winnowers and huskers. Electrically powered corn
mills are used for flour production.

Communes with electricity provide supplies to
individual houses for lighting, with both incandescent and
fluorescent lamps,and to drive fans. Meeting halls have
lighting, record players, film projectors and public address
systems. In some there are also television receivers.

VII CROPS

Because of great climatic diversity China is able to
produce a wide variety of crops including food grains, oil
seeds, pulses, root crops, vegetables, fruits and nuts,
and non-food plants.

1. **Food Grains** : The principal food grains are rice,
wheat, millet, maize, sorghum, barley, and oats. Annual
production is put usually at 240×10^6 tons but this includes

an allowance for sweet potato and similar vegetables.

(a) Rice

Rice is grown, in some 20 varieties, throughout Agricultural China, from the Canton area in the South to the latitude of Peking in the North, and in the Szechuan basin.

Rice paddy fields, on alluvial plains or terraced hillsides, are prepared by puddling using water buffalo or other draught animals. With increasing mechanisation tractors are now being introduced. Seedlings transplanted from nursery seed beds are set at high densities. The usual density is such that 120 kg of seed rice, germinated in 1 ha, is transplanted to 8 or 10 ha of paddy field. The crop grows very densely and is weeded regularly; there is little lodging to cause harvesting difficulties. Transplanting is almost universal in China and enables two or three crops to be produced annually. The preferred rotation is two rice crops, taking 75 and 90 days respectively, and one of wheat, taking 105 days. In some areas all three crops are rice.

Organic manures of human, animal and compost origin are spread before planting at rates of between 22500 kg/ha to 37500 kg/ha. Immediately prior to transplanting 20% ammonia solution is applied at the rate of 750 kg/ha.

Production figures for the various Communes visited showed great variation, because of climatic and physical conditions, but all showed significant production gains since liberation :-

Da Li Commune, Canton - a rich Commune specialising in rice production.

> Husked Rice
>
> | | | |
> |---|---|---|
> | Average yield | 1953-1957 | 4650 kg/ha |
> | Annual yield | 1958 | 6220 kg/ha |
> | Annual yield | 1963 | 8250 kg/ha |
> | Annual yield | 1970 | 9900 kg/ha |

- in terms of paddy, rice in husk after threshing, the 1970 figure represents about 14000 kg/ha from three crops in the year.

<u>San Tsun Production Team, Canton</u> - in a relatively poor Commune

<u>Paddy</u>

Annual yield   1958   2250 kg/ha

Annual yield   1971   6750 kg/ha

<u>Sino-Cuban Commune, Peking</u> - grows wheat with some rice

<u>Paddy</u>

Annual yield   1949   750 kg/ha

Annual yield   1971   8250 kg/ha

<u>'July 1st' Commune, Shanghai</u>

<u>Rotation : 2 crops rice and 1 crop wheat in 1971</u>

Annual yield   1950   3300 kg/ha

Annual yield   1957   4400 kg/ha

Annual yield   1971   11400 kg/ha (Rice + Wheat)

- other rotations in use include 2 crops of rice a year for two years followed by one year of cotton. Within this Commune an advanced Brigade produces an average of 15000 kg/ha of rice and wheat. A backward Brigade produces only 10000 kg/ha.

<u>Ho La Commune, Wusih</u>

Paddy

Annual yield   1948   3400 kg/ha (pre-liberation)

Annual yield   1953(?)   4650 kg/ha (Ag. Co-op Movement)

Annual yield   1958   6000 kg/ha (Peoples Commune)

Annual yield   1971   8250 kg/ha

- formerly 2 rice crops now 2 of rice and 1 of wheat. Green manure, fishpond silt and 600 kg/ha artificial fertiliser now used.

(b) Wheat

The greatest wheat producing areas are in the north of Agricultural China although the rice growing areas grow considerable quantities of wheat as a third crop. The seed rate for wheat is high also, up to 200 kg/ha, with fertilizer rates of about 4500 kg/ha. The fertilizer is 90% organic and 10% ammonium sulphate. Harvesting is still largely manual, however a variety of mechanical aids including some combine harvesters have been introduced. Average yields have increased considerably since liberation :-

Sino-Cuban Commune, Peking

Wheat

Annual yield	1949	800 kg/ha
Annual yield	1971	5400 kg/ha
Annual yield	1972	6000 kg/ha

Ho La Commune, Wusih

Wheat, single crop

Annual yield	1948	675 kg/ha
Annual yield	1953(?)	1600 kg/ha
Annual yield	1958	2400 kg/ha
Annual yield	1971	3800 kg/ha

- in 1971 the total yield from 2 crops of rice and 1 of wheat was about 12000 kg/ha.

(c) Millet, Maize and Sorghum

Millet and sorghum are grown in the drier parts of China to the north of the Hwang Ho. Maize is grown north of the Yangtse. Some of these coarse grains are for human consumption but most of the production is used to feed stock or is fermented to produce alcoholic drinks.

2. <u>Oil Seeds and Pulses</u> : Groundnuts and mustard, grown throughout China, provide oil for cooking and for export. Rape, colza, soya, linseed, cottonseed, teaseed, sesame, sunflowerseed and palm oils are produced in suitable areas as are olive, castor and coconut oils. Many of these are offered as export commodities along with tung oil.

Groundnuts (peanuts) are grown widely as a field crop and on private plots in the relatively dry areas; after the nuts are gathered the leaves and stems are dug in as fertilizer.

For a long time soya bean has been the principal source of protein for the Chinese people. It is grown wherever possible, eaten in many forms and, as fermented bean ourd, is used in the preparation of many Chinese dishes. Until recently animal protein was scarce and despite great efforts to increase pig raising, fish farming and dairy herds, the majority of people in China are dependent on soya for their protein intake. Total soya bean production is estimated to be 12×10^6 tons per annum; a large part is converted to soya flour or to cattle cake after the oil has been extracted.

Many other kinds of beans and peas are grown for human or animal consumption or as fertilizers. Green beans are a particularly common dietary item.

3. <u>Root Crops</u> : Sweet potato is the cheapest staple food in China and is grown extensively. Other roots generally available are carrot, turnip, sugar beet, yam, cassava (manioc or arrow root), Irish potato, and Taro-root.

Sweet potato is very important as a survival crop when the other staples are in short supply. In ordinary times it is used to feed pigs and poultry and is grown commonly on the private plots of Commune members. Two varieties are grown, with white or yellow flesh. The former has the better storage qualities.

4. Vegetables and other edible plants : Chinese cabbage, cabbage, onion, leek, garlic, spinach, tomato, cucumber, capsicum, egg-plant, ginger and bamboo shoot are all available and commonly eaten in Chinese dishes. The "July 1st" Commune near Shanghai produces vegetables for the city market and has obtained considerable increases in production since the establishment of the Commune :-

Average yield of vegetables	1950	17000 kg/ha
Average yield of vegetables	1957	21500 kg/ha
Average yield of vegetables	1971	75000 kg/ha

Water chestnut, water oats, lotus and water hyacinth are grown in swampy areas and shallow waterways. The seeds of lotus are eaten and the leaves and stalks fed to pigs or composted. Water hyacinth, a waterway pest in many parts of the world, is grown extensively as a nutritive pig food; it is eaten also by water buffalo.

Water chestnut and the underwater shoots of water oats are commonly gathered by girls who sit in floating tubs and paddle along using their hands.

5. Fruits and Nuts : An extensive range of fruits are grown in China although in quantities insufficient to meet present demand. Specialised fruit tree research institutes are providing new varieties of apple, pear, melon, peach, grape and persimmon. Many excellent named varieties are grown; in addition to seeking increased yields, work is directed toward lengthening the fruit harvesting season at each end and toward varieties with better keeping properties.

Other fruits include apricot, plums of several kinds, cherry, banana, various kinds of orange, mango, pineapple, pawpaw, pomegranate, gourds, guava, cumquat, longan, lychee and coconut.

Gourds are grown along the edge of irrigation channels and the stems are trained on to flat bamboo frames, supported on poles, over the water.

6. Other Plants : Sugar cane is grown extensively but refined sugar is not an important dietary item.

Tea is the most important beverage shrub, cocoa and coffee are also grown. There is a wide range of tea varieties, black, green and red, grown in different parts of the country.

7. **Non-food Plants** : China produces a wide range of vegetable products for industry including rubber and tobacco. The most important fibres are cotton, ramies, hemp, jute and flax. Cotton is grown often as a crop in a rice/cotton rotation. Yields of gin cotton have increased considerably since the Shanghai "July 1st" Commune was established :-

Average yield of gin cotton	1950	170 kg/ha
Average yield of gin cotton	1957	410 kg/ha
Average yield of gin cotton	1971	785 kg/ha

- on this Commune cotton growing land is fertilized by organic matter with the addition of ammonium phosphate and nitrogenous chemical fertilizers.

VIII ANIMAL HUSBANDRY

Apart from pigs China has a relatively small animal production. The major protein requirement is met from vegetable sources, mainly soya bean; milk consumption is confined to young children and invalids. The principal sources of animal protein are pork and eggs. Efforts are being made to increase the stock of pigs, cattle, sheep, chickens and "Peking ducks". Horses, donkeys, mules, oxen and water buffalo are used extensively as draught animals.

1. **Pigs** : Many Communes have one or more Pig Farms; sweet potato and water hyacinth are grown as pig food. Almost all families fatten one or two pigs, bought as piglets, from the Commune and sold full grown to supplement family income. Special encouragement to increase pig stocks has been given by Chairman Mao's call for everyone to raise one pig. Numbers have increased and parity with the human population has been attained in some Communes:

Da Li Commune, Canton - (63000 persons)

Cross bred pigs - Danish white and Chinese Grey variety.

Pig population : 20000 (1948); 60000 (1970); 62000 (1972)

Pigs housed in extremely clean brick pens; heavily treated with insecticide, few flies.

Sino-Cuban Commune, Peking - (38000 persons)

Black pigs, a chinese variety.

Pig population : 26000 (6000 sent to City markets annually)

"July 1st" Commune, Shanghai - (16836 persons)

Pig population : 2000 (1950); 4000 (1957); 22000 (1972)

2. Cattle and Horses : Water buffalo and oxen remain the primary source of power for heavy field work on the rice producing Communes. Dairy herds have been started in many parts of the country with black-and-white Friesian cattle originally introduced from the Netherlands.

(a) Water buffalo

Two varieties of water buffalo are bred in China. The common draught animal, black with curved horns, and the brown buffalo, with straight horns, which produces high butter fat (12 - 14%) milk. The latter is found in the southern parts of the country.

(b) Horses

Horse farms are an important feature in the northern parts of China where horses are the principal draught animals, for farm and carters' work, and as a means of communication where all-weather roads and mechanical transport have not been established. In Communes near Peking horses outnumbered dairy cattle.

3. Poultry and Ducks : Many Commune farms are devoted
to chickens and ducks. Most peasant families keep several
chickens and a two or three ducks to provide eggs for daily
consumption. Much attention is paid to poultry and duck
rearing; well designed rotating drum hatching cabinets and
several different types of incubators are used to aid high
rates of hatching (over 90%) and rearing. Houses are simply
constructed from cheap local materials and are kept very
clean.

Communes near the larger cities have special duck farms
to meet the growing demand for "Peking" duck. Ducks are fed
liberally for 30 to 40 days after which they are forced fed,
on a mixture of grain and soya meal with additives, for
another 20 days. In this way rearing time is reduced and
table weight increased to about 2.5 kg, about 1 kg over
natural weight.

IX FISH FARMING

Fresh water fishing in lakes and rivers is practised
throughout China. All reservoirs are stocked with fish.
Fish Farming has a long history in China and, since the
establishment of Communes, has greatly extended in the Yangtse
and Sikiang basins.

Ho La Commune near Wusih, in the lake country south
of the Yangtse in Kiangsu Province, has over 100 ha of
fishponds. The brigade visited has three fish-farming
Production Teams working 162 fishponds with a total area of
42 ha. Before liberation these ponds were owned and operated
by fish lords. Most were shallow and produced less fish than
the deeper ponds. After the establishment of the Commune
deepening of all the ponds was started and, over seven years,
some 900000 m^3 of silt were removed and the average depth
increased from 1.5 to 3.6 m. The silt was used to improve
land for the planting of Mulberry trees. The ponds are
mostly rectangular with bottoms sloping from end to end to
facilitate fishing by drag nets and to provide refuge for
the fish if the water level falls. It has been found that
the optimum size of pond for fish production is between

0.25 and 0.4 ha; most ponds are about 0.25 ha in area.

The ponds are enriched with pig manure, silk-worm pupae, snails, sweet potato leaves. Some seven different species of fish feed on this material, water vegetation and plankton. Fish are selected to include species which live in each of the lower, middle and upper layers of the pond. Fishponds are cleaned every two or three years and the dredged material used as fertilizer. Young fish (fry) are introduced in to the ponds in February and fed on a well ground mixture of 95% beancake with 5% soya bean; the first fish are taken for eating in July. The ponds are then fished three or four times a year, throughout the useful life of the pond. The largest fish take three years to reach full size with individual weights up to 8 kg. Fish production has risen since the deepened ponds became productive and now exceeds 8000 kg per annum per hectare of water surface:

1948	3750 kg/ha	Pre-liberation
1953 (?)	5250 kg/ha	Ag. Co-op. Movement
1958	6000 kg/ha	People's Commune
1971	8250 kg/ha	

Some fish disease has occurred but has not reached epidemic proportions. No oxygen deficiency problems have been encountered. Water beetles which wound fish, are controlled by spraying 666(Benzene hexachloride) on to the water surface. The dosage was found by experiment and is believed to be harmless to fish.

In some ponds cultured pearls are grown in shell-fish (scallops) tethered on long lines.

X   SERICULTURE

China has been a producer of silk since ancient times; it is still the world's major producer and continues to meet a steady world demand.   . Within China silk is expensive and is available in competition with much cheaper 'dacron'.

White silk, from Kiangsu, Chekiang, and Kwangtung, and yellow silk from Shangtung and Szechuan, are produced from the cocoons of silkworm pupae raised on mulberry leaves. Coarser wild silk is made from the cocoons of silkworms raised on the leaves of the chestnut-leaved oak. Another coarse variety of silk is obtained from silkworms fed on Cassava leaves.

At Ho La Commune, near Wusih in South Kiangsu, silkworms are reared by Production Teams as a side-line occupation for women workers. On this Commune there are 53 ha of mulberry trees. The Brigade visited had 22 ha of mulberry grown on land enriched with silt from fishponds. Traditionally mulberry trees were grown at a density of 4200 per hectare. After some experimentation by Commune members a greater yield of leaves is obtained now by close planting, in rows one metre apart and with a separation in the rows of about 80 cm., at a density of 12000 trees per hectare. The silkworms are raised in a large airy shed (cocoonery). After the eggs have hatched the larvae are placed on flat circular woven trays or baskets where they are fed on finely chopped mulberry leaves. These trays are stacked in well separated vertical racks to ensure uniform temperature and adequate ventilation. From the laying of an egg by the female moth, through hatching and larval stages, to the spinning of the cocoon takes between 20 and 30 days. In the past two crops of cocoons were produced annually but now four or five are possible. Since liberation the output of cocoons per hectare of mulberry trees has more than doubled :-

1948	340 kg/ha	Pre-liberation
1953(?)	490 kg/ha	Ag. Co-op. Movement
1958	600 kg/ha	Peoples Commune
1971	760 kg/ha	

Wusih is a centre of white silk production and cocoons raised on the Communes are taken to silk-reeling mills (filatures) where silk yarn is made up from the threads from 7 or 8 cocoons; each cocoon gives 600 m to 800 m of thread. Cocoon residues are retained for use as fish food or in pharmaceutical preparations.

A visit was paid to the Wusih No.1 Silk Reeling Mill.
This mill is 40 years old and employs 1700 workers, 80% women,
many of whom started as child labour and have worked in the
mill for over 20 years. The process starts with the sorting
of the cocoons; those of acceptable quality are vacuum boiled,
melting the silk paste to release the thread ends, and then
taken to the reeling machines. The mill has vertical reelers
developed by the workers; a manual reeler that can take 28
thread ends is being replaced by an automatic 60-end reeler.
The yarn, re-reeled and dried to ensure good storage qualities,
is then skeined and bundled for despatch. The colour, gauge
and strength of the yarn samples are assessed to ensure that
the product meets the standards of the international market.

XI NON-AGRICULTURAL PRODUCTION

The call for Communes to emphasise self-reliance and self-
sufficiency, exemplified by the slogan "walking-on-two-legs",
has had great impact on China's countryside and most Communes
now have a workshop and some manufacturing facilities. Some
attempts to reproduce complex processes, on the Commune, in the
absence of adequate skills and process controls had to be
abandoned. With experience gained most Communes have been able
to establish a number of effective production units and efforts
to further the ideal of self-sufficiency continue.

Every Commune and State Farm has blacksmith and metal-
working shops where simple farm tools are made and repaired.
With the introduction of tractors and irrigation pumps
workshops have expanded their range of skills so that the new
items of equipment may be repaired. Communes now have
technicians and skilled workers able to conceive and construct
tools and equipment to meet special needs. On many Communes
great efforts are being made to make effective rice-
transplanters and harvesters as existing models are
unsatisfactory. As designs become more complex Commune
workshops are acquiring a variety of machine tools for grinding,
drilling and turning. Such expansion of facilities has been
greatly simplified by the spread of three-phase electric power
supplies to the countryside. The principal use of electricity
is to drive irrigation pumps and some Commune workshops are
able to assemble or part-fabricate pumps and electric motors.

Brickworks, cement works, limestone quarries and quarries for extracting phosphatic rocks are operated where possible. Coal briquettes for cooking fires are made from bulk delivered low grade coal dust. Small plants are built, on many Communes, to produce ammonia, the most widely used artificial fertilizer. Commune insecticide and pesticide factories process and dilute concentrated materials obtained from the growing petro-chemical industry; some Communes also produce plant based insecticides. Medicinal plants are commonly grown and supplied to Commune clinics and pharmacies, and to City users of indigenous medicines.

Food processing, such as grain milling, rice polishing and the extraction of cooking oils from seeds is carried out on all Communes to meet local consumers' needs. Some specialised Commune factories process or preserve vegetables and fruits for export.

Commune shoe and clothing factories produce goods of everyday quality for local consumption or undertake sub-contract work for factories in towns. Toys, ornaments, pottery, basket work, textile embroidery and other craft products are sold, to town shops, to enhance the cash income of the Commune. Knitted and crocheted articles are made and sold by women members of Commune families.

Farm buildings, workshops and houses are built by specialised Production Teams using the largest amount possible of locally produced materials.

XII SOCIAL CONDITIONS IN THE COMMUNES

The 78000 Communes of China function over an immense range of climates and terrains and any conclusions, on any aspect of such a complex society, made during a brief visit are obviously suspect. In reading the following comments the fact that they are based on visits to only five Communes should be borne in mind.

1. Working Population : As is to be expected in a society that has seen a large growth in population in recent times the population appears young. The structures of six households visited are :-

FAMILY 'A'   Tung Fang Commune, Canton

(Man, head of household   : Worker in Production Team
(Wife   : Worker in Production Team

(Eldest Son   (aged 25) : Teacher in Primary School
(Daughter-in-law   : Worker in Production Team

Elder Daughter   (aged 24) : Worker in Production Team

Second Son   (aged 20) : Worker in Commune

Younger Daughter   (aged 18) : High School Student

Third Son   (aged 8) : Primary School Student
   - and two infant grandchildren

(This family lives in two houses)

FAMILY 'B'   Tung Fang Commune, Canton

(Man, head of household   : Worker in Production Team
(Wife   : Worker in Production Team

Eldest Son   (aged 18) : Bridge building labourer

Second Son   (aged 15) : Middle School Student

Third Son   (aged 10) : Primary School Student

(A daughter aged 21 is married and lives with her husband's family).

FAMILY 'C'   Sino-Cuban Commune, Peking

(Man, head of household   : Worker in Production Team
(Wife   : Worker in Production Team

Elder Son   (aged 6) : Primary School Student

Daughter   (aged 3) : attends Kindergarten

Younger Son   (aged 1) : attends Kindergarten

FAMILY 'D'   Sino-Cuban Commune, Peking

A household of 8 with 4 able-bodied farm workers. Family has four generations living together. The youngest child is just over one year old and his great-grandmother is 78.

FAMILY 'E'   Ho La Commune, Wusih

(Man   (aged 26) : Member of Fishing Production Team
(Wife   (aged 26) : Works in side-line shoe factory

Mother, head of household (aged 49) : Worker in side-line cocoonery

Sister   (aged 20) : Worker in Production Team

Three Younger Brothers   : Workers in Production Team

Youngest Brother   : at School

FAMILY 'F'   "July 1st" Commune, Shanghai

(Man, head of household : Dock worker
(Wife   : Worker in Production Team

Mother   : past retirement age

(Son   : Worker in farm tool workshop
(Daughter-in-law   : Worker in livestock Production Team
(Grandson (aged 2+)   : under school age

Daughter   : Worker in Production Team

Details of the circumstances of these families are given in TABLE II on a following page.

There is some confusion, in the information given on the Communes, between families and households. Households including married sons or daughters with their wives or husbands and children appear to be considered as multi-family households. The following figures are based on families :-

"July 1st" Commune

Population : 16836   Families : 4122   Workers : 9900

Number of persons per family (average) : 4.1

Percentage of able-bodied workers   : 59%

TABLE II : SIX COMMUNE FAMILIES

Family	A	B	C	D	E	F
Commune	Tung Fang	Tung Fang	Sino-Cuban	Sino-Cuban	Ho La	"July 1st"
District	Canton	Canton	Peking	Peking	Wusih	Shanghai
Family Size (including infants)	10	5	5	8	8	7
Workers	6	3	2	4(7)*	4	5
Income :						
Including kind (£)	780	500	350	570*	580	1200
Cash (£)	210	260	130	260*	370	
Private Plot (£)		90				160
House :						
Date built	1967	1965			(old)	1952
Cost (£)	1100	390				
Electricity supply	✓	✓	✓	✓	✓	✓
Consumption :						
Daily grain (kg)	7.5		3	5	3.5	3
Yearly grain/capita (kg)	280		220	230	160	160
Weekly Fish	daily	3+	daily	main dishes weekly	daily	3
Weekly Meat (Pork)	3 or 4	1 or 2	if wanted		1 or 2	3
Daily eggs	✓	✓	✓	✓	✓	✓
Household goods :						
Sewing machine	2	1	1	1	0	
Bicycle	2+	2		✓	2	
Watch or Clock	1	2		✓	2	
Radio			1	1	0	
Fan	1	1				
Private Plot :						
Size (m²)	330	180	(for 300 kg) grain	(for 500 kg) grain	100	330
Pigs	14	2	2	2	0	0
Hens/Chickens	33	15	10	10	4	4
Ducks	31	10			3	3

* Family D : Seven members of the family work. Four in Production Teams obtained the income given in the table. The earnings of two working in sideline occupations, and one at School in 1971, but now working, have not been included.

Brigade in Ho La Commune

Population : 3962   Families : 986   Workers : 1852

    Number of persons per family (average) : 4.0

    Percentage of able-bodied workers   : 47%

On several occasions it was explained that 55% of workers are women. Some residents of the Commune, mostly men, may work outside in nearby factories.

2.   Income : The pay of farm workers on Communes is based on a daily work points system. The total work points are the product of the number of days worked and the work point rating of the worker. Work points differ between different Production Teams, and between different Communes, depending on the Productive success and wealth of the each Team. Pay reflects local conditions including the quality of management by the various Revolutionary Committees. Workers and Cadres, mostly Party members, are said to receive pay on the same basis, but there is evidence that work point ratings reflect political consciousness and ideological integrity. This approach has been repudiated from the top but appears to persist in some Communes. Old and infirm people work when they are able. If any family has too few able-bodied workers, to provide an adequate income, welfare funds in the Commune are used to ensure a minimum family living standard.

On the "July 1st" Commune work point allocation reflects the principles that "All should work for the public interest" and "Pay should be for work done". The skill, physical condition of the worker and his attitude towards product quality and public interest are taken into account. Work points are proposed by Production Team members after discussion within the Team, and are subject to the approval of the Team Revolutionary Committee. Women and men receive equal ratings for the same work but heavy jobs, such as carrying loads on shoulder poles, carry high ratings and are performed by men. On average women are rated at 9.5 work points compared with 11 for men as most women are engaged on light jobs such as weeding and digging vegetables.

On Ho La Commune a woman working in a side-line shoe factory was rated at 7.7 work points and was paid in the same way as Production Team field workers. Workers in factories that are Commune enterprises are paid a wage in the same way as industrial workers.

Most Communes calculate pay for field workers on the basis that 10 work points, a work-day, are paid at a rate between 1.0 and 1.30 yuan. Earnings of able-bodied field workers, compiled from data from the five Communes visited, are shown in Table III. These earnings are from Commune agricultural activities and do not include income from private plots or from raising and selling private pigs. From 50% to 75% of income is taken in the form of grain, oil and other necessities; the balance in cash. The proportions of income taken in cash and kind for several families are shown in Table IV.

Since the establishment of People's Communes incomes have increased considerably. For example, the average annual household income on "July 1st" Commune was 110 yuan ($48) in 1950, 365 yuan ($160) in 1957 and 770 yuan ($330) in 1971. During that period grain and other household essentials have not changed in price. From 1962 to 1972 the value of 10 work points on the Sino-Cuban Commune has increased from 0.178 yuan to 1.28 yuan. Low work point values are now seen to be feature of a situation in which excessive attention is attached to the accumulation of work points and insufficient to the quality of the product.

Workers in Communes have 8 hour day, in two four hour shifts, but this is reduced to 6 hours or less during slack periods. At harvest times peasants are joined by industrial workers and soldiers; long hours are worked to clear the harvest and replant the next crop.

Full-time workers in Commune factories and similar enterprises work 8 hours a day for six days a week. Pay tends to be higher than for agricultural work and averages about 500 yuan ($220) per annum. Workers in Commune factories have private plots and take part in agricultural work during busy seasons of the year. In comparison, workers in a cement-boat factory in Wusih are paid on an eight-point scale ranging from 380 yuan per annum ($160) for Grade 1 apprentices to 1100 yuan per annum ($550) for a highly skilled and responsible

TABLE III : ANNUAL EARNINGS OF ABLE-BODIED FIELD WORKERS

(from Commune funds only)

Commune	10 workpoints equivalent (yuan)	Individual earnings - cash and kind		
		maximum (yuan)	average (yuan)	minimum (yuan)
Da Li Canton	1.10 or 1.20	550		250
Tung Fang Canton	1.0	450		250
Sino-Cuban Peking	1.28	600	300+	300-
Ho La Wusih	1.12	520 -560		320 -360
"July 1st" Shanghai	*(1.25)	(500)	(370 -490)	(270)

* assumed figure   N.B. £ 1 = 2.3 yuan

- -

TABLE IV : CASH AND KIND IN FIELD WORKERS ANNUAL INCOME

(private plot and side-line income excluded)

Family	A	B	C	D	E
Commune Household Size Workers	Tung Fang 10 6	Tung Fang 5 3	Sino-Cuban 5 2	Sino-Cuban 8 4	Ho La 8 *4
Income : Total Kind Cash	yuan % 1800 (100) 1310 (73) 480 (27)	yuan % 1150 (100) 550 (48) 600 (52)	yuan % 800 (100) 500 (63) 300 (37)	yuan % 1300 (100) 700 (54) 600 (46)	yuan % 1330 (100) 850 (64) 480 (36)

* Two other family members work in side-line occupations

Grade 9 worker; most workers are in Grades 3 to 5 and receive from 540 to 750 yuan per annum (£230 to 330). In a major state engineering factory in Shanghai pay, also on an eight-point scale for post-apprentice employees, ranged from 500 to 1500 yuan per annum (£220 to 660) with a plant average of over 800 yuan per annum (£350).

There is no state tax on personal incomes in China. State revenue is obtained from the profits of state industries and from taxes on industrial goods and agricultural production. There are also taxes on cigarettes and alcoholic drinks. The agricultural tax amounts to 5 or 6% of gross agricultural production.

Family savings out of income are generally earmarked for housing or consumers' goods. Annual savings of from 50 to 500 yuan (£22 to 220) were mentioned by Commune members. Savings are deposited with the People's Bank; short term deposits receive interest at the rate of 1.4% per annum, longer term receive 1.8%.

3.   Housing : All houses on Communes are privately owned; many have been built in recent years. They are austere, lacking interior plasterwork or surface finishes, but everyone appeared adequately housed. Village layouts are very variable; traditional villages have often a more open aspect and enclosed gardens. New houses on reclaimed land are cramped and enclosed in an effort to minimise the use of land that would otherwise be agriculturally productive.

Houses are built by specialised production teams and financed by the savings of Commune members. The price for a modest three-roomed house, of fired bricks and other local materials, with attached kitchen ranged from 500 to 900 yuan (£220 to 390); 2500 yuan (£1100) had been paid for a house with five large rooms, kitchen and yard.

All the houses visited used straw, supplemented by coal briquettes, for cooking and water boiling. Near Peking houses have brick sleeping platforms - Kangs, heated internally by hot flue gases from the kitchen fire.

4.   Consumers' Goods : Commune members have a wide
choice of household goods in village shops. The purchase of
larger items may require a visit to shops and stores in the
larger towns. Distributive agencies are all state controlled
and sell at fixed prices.

All families visited had cups or drinking glasses, bowls,
chopsticks, enamel ware, pots and pans; also toothbrushes,
often with foaming toothpaste, soap and facecloths. Furniture
included chairs, stools, tables, beds, cupboards and shelves.
Each house had one or more giant vacuum-flasks for water,
boiled in the morning, to be kept hot all day for drinking or
for making tea. Boiled water is the everyday drink throughout
China; tea is something of a luxury.

Almost every household has one or more bicycles, the
ubiquitous means of transport in China - there are an
estimated two million bicycles in Peking. Most households
have treddle sewing machines, often with specially designed
sewing tables. Many households have clocks, wrist-watches,
transistor radio sets and electric fans. All the houses on
the Communes visited had unshaded electric lights. While
travelling many houses were seen to have electricity supplies.

The 72 households of San Tsun Village Production Team,
near Canton, own 79 bicycles, 49 sewing machines and 38 radio
sets.

Living room wall decorations, include coloured posters,
such as portraits of Chairman Mao and scenes from the
revolutionary operas and ballets, and family photographs.

Most clothing is cotton though other fabrics are available.
The well known blue jacket-and-trouser suit is the basis of
everyday clothing but many individual variations are seen.
Many men now wear cotton and dacron shirts and women coloured
and patterned blouses. Children have a wide range of clothing
styles and patterns; from floral prints to 'mickey-mouse'
shirts. Sandals are the common form of foot wear. Shoes are
sold in city shops. On the Communes field workers usually
go barefooted.

5.   Leisure : Leisure time activities include evening
attendance at political and production team meetings. Most
Commune members attend one or two evening meetings each week,
but an active cadre and Party member is expected to attend
five or six. Local and national newspapers are available
and usually read in groups at breaks in the working day. Wall
newspapers are a common feature of Communes, factories and
schools. Books are scarce. Most houses have the selected
works of Mao Tse-tung, the pamphlets 'Serve the People',
'The Foolish Old Man who Moved Mountains' and 'In Memory of
Dr. Norman Bethune'. A few houses had technical or farming
handbooks.

Entertainment includes watching television in Team or
Commune headquarters and listening to personal radios or
broadcasts relayed through the Commune loudspeaker system.
Mobile film and shadow puppetry units visit Production Teams.
Schoolchildren sing and demonstrate 'national minority'
dances. All forms of entertainment are educational or have
revolutionary or ideological content.

Inviting friends to take tea and to join in conversation
was mentioned often as a leisure activity. Other activities
included taking family members into town to look at the stores,
attend cinema performances, or to try new dishes at restaurants.

Bookshops in cities are well stocked with the works of
Marx, Engels, Lenin, Stalin and Mao Tse-tung and with many
cheap and comprehensive technical handbooks. A small bookshop
in Shanghai had a range of new and second-hand copies of the
Chinese classics which were unobtainable during the more
puritanical phase of the Chinese revolution.

Near the cities shops, parks and national monuments are
popular for rest day, usually Sunday, family outings. In
Peking, the Forbidden City, Tien An Men square, the Summer
Palace, the Temple of Heaven and the Zoo are crowded on
Sundays. Longer group excursions are made from Peking to the
Great Wall, the Ming Tombs and the Underground Palace
(Ting Ling).

The common forms of physical excercise in the Communes
are basket ball, table tennis and traditional excercises.

6.   Schools : Communes have their own educational
systems with primary and middle schools. All children in the
areas visited received primary education, many went on to
junior middle school with a lesser number completing middle
school. The Sino-Cuban Commune, near Peking, has a population
of 38000 served by 15 primary and 3 middle schools. The Da Li
Commune, near Canton, has a population of 63000, 20 village
primary schools with a total of 54 middle school classes and
a Commune high school; student numbers have increased from
2000 before liberation to 10700.

Subjects taught include reading and writing Chinese,
mathematics, Maoist thought, science, art and practical
subjects related to the work of the Commune. Learning by
rote was a feature of the classes seen in action.

Foreign languages are taught from the fourth primary
year; Russian is now superseded by English as the principal
language taught.

Education in China is not free but the fees of 4 yuan
per year for primary level and 8 yuan for middle school amount
to a very small part of the cash earnings of Commune families.

7.   Health and Welfare : China has a medical system
which provides essential preventative and clinical services to
the whole population.

The Communes have their own 20 or 30 bed hospitals with
fully trained doctors practising both 'indigenous' and
'western' medicine. Such hospitals are equipped to perform
minor surgical operations as well as treating more serious
medical cases including maternity complications. Within the
Commune, Brigade level clinics, staffed by experienced medical
technicians, dispense all type of medicines and provide
maternity services. Such clinics often have herb gardens in
which a wide range of remedial plants are grown. Each
Production Team has a medical technician, called a "Barefoot
Doctor", who can deal with minor ailments and accidents.

Barefoot doctors spend part of their time on medical duties and part as ordinary field workers. They are given six-months basic instruction followed by periods of in-practice training under the supervision of more experienced technicians. The barefoot doctor has a small health centre with stocks of traditional herbal and 'western' medicines, simple surgical instruments, acupuncture needles and charts, and a first-aid field bag.

In China great emphasis is placed on preventative medicine and the barefoot doctor instructs Team members in hygiene and child care, as well as vaccinating infants against smallpox and spraying houses with insecticides. In addition the barefoot doctor advises on contraception and is a member of the Team family planning propaganda team.

The health centre holds stocks of B.C.G., and cholera vaccine. Tubercolosis and venereal diseases, once common in China, have been virtually eliminated. In the Shanghai area there are still some cases of shistosomiasis and on the "July 1st" Commune the present incidence was said to be 5%; at the time of liberation it was about 50%.

The practice of boiling all drinking water, universal in China, is effective in controlling water borne disease. Common ailments on Communes are the common cold, and diarrhoea in children. There are some cases of intestinal worms. Nutritional deficiency diseases are uncommon but bottles of Vitamin B pills were seen in several of the houses visited.

The medical staff of the "July 1st" Commune near Shanghai, with the aid of the County medical authorities, had carried out recently a full medical examination of all married women up to the age of sixty. Of some 5000 women examined two were found to have cancer of the cervix; other gynaecological complaints were also diagnosed.

The Da Li Commune, near Canton, with a population of 63000 has a central hospital, two sub-clinics and 195 medical personnel, including 59 barefoot doctors.

Specialist treatment is available in County and City hospitals and the cost of such treatment is borne by Commune funds. All Commune members pay about two yuan each year for treatment rights under a co-operative medical system.

Industrial workers and foreign residents have similar medical insurance. Foreign visitors are not charged for the treatment of minor ailments but hospital treatment of serious illness is expensive.

In rural areas the age of retirement is 60 for men and 55 for women. Pensions are paid from welfare funds. There are homes for old people, but in a country with strong family ties most old people live with married sons or daughters. Grandmothers, in particular, play an important part in family life; they are often the family banker and look after young children when the able-bodied members of the family are at work.

8. <u>Mobility</u> : In all developing countries the drift of population from the land to the city is a serious social problem exacerbated by mechanisation reducing agricultural labour. The drift in China has been reversed. Social and political pressures encourage the establishment of light industries in the countryside. Such industries absorb former agricultural workers and contribute to self-reliance within the Communes. During the period of the Cultural Revolution many young educated people were sent to the Communes; many remain in the countryside, others have returned to urban employment. To emphasise the 'equality' of agricultural, industrial and bureaucratic employment, urban workers are expected to spend part of each year working with the peasants on the Communes.

9. <u>Rationing</u> : Food grains, for personal consumption, and cotton cloth, for home clothes making, are rationed in China. The grain ration is presently more than adequate; the rationing system is maintained to deal with any shortages, such as harvest failures, that might occur. Textile production is increasing; rationing restricts the demand for piece goods which can not yet be met fully. Off-ration clothing, in a variety of natural and artificial textiles, is available in the stores but is relatively expensive.

Ration cards are honoured only in the district of issue unless transfer is authorised.

XIII CONCLUSIONS

Impressions of China are inevitably subjective, especially as comparative statistical data is lacking. The Government of the People's Republic has not published the population, production and investment statistics, which are taken for granted in other parts of the world; it is possible that such information has not been collected on any regular basis.

There is no doubt that China is a remarkably egalitarian society even though examples of inequality and differential incentives can be adduced. This egalitarianism is a by-product of policies rather than a desired end. On several occasions Commune members quoted socialist guidelines, such as "He who does not work shall not eat" and "From each according to his ability and to each according to his contribution", and indicated that following the achievements of Tachai Commune was the way to overcome their difficulties. Simple equal distribution unrelated to production is dismissed as "Left-wing Communism".

The benefits for the peasant and farm worker of a society that provides adequate minimum food, housing and social security are obvious. The price of such benefits is real, too. In the short term, the growth of industry, already supporting a large armaments burden, has been relatively slow due to capital shortages. This may have repercussions in a society where many members see the availability of consumers' goods as an index of progress. The rate of acquisition of bicycles, sewing machines, wrist-watches and radios is a matter of pride amongst Commune members. No one considers any of these items as undesirable but, as 'Western' society well knows, consumer pressures are insidious if not inevitable. In China the savings of Commune members, amounting to 20% or more of gross agricultural production, represent a potential consumers' pressure that Chinese society and Maoist ideology will have to face. At the present time television sets are bought by Communes; works of art are not - or not yet.

Accepting that the future is unclear, there is no doubt that the progress of the People's Republic has been one of steady achievement since the three bad harvests of 1959, 1960 and 1961. Production, self-reliance, and crop and stock improvements have all advanced. The mass of the population of rural China accepts the rule of the Communist Party, which has greatly reduced the possibility of widespread flood or famine, and has provided adequate food, housing and basic social services.

The impact of adequate supplies of electric power to the Communes will accelerate new social changes started by the introduction of the walking tractor and simple mechanisation.

The development of the Commune is one of the most important social experiments of the present time. The division of non-industrial China into 78000 semi-autonomous Communes has provided China with a solution to problems that also affect other parts of the world :-

(a) Communes, with their sub-divisions of Brigades and Production Teams, provide the individual peasant with a living and working unit which he can comprehend, with which he can identify himself, and in which he has a reasonable chance of participating in management.

(b) Self-reliance, in agriculture and everyday necessities, and the establishment of local factories enhance local autonomy and reduce demands for capital investment in distributive transport.

(c) In the event of nuclear warfare Chinese society, in autonomous and autarchic Communes, is much more likely to survive than highly integrated and inter-dependent economic systems.

Is China a good example for other poor countries to follow? The organisation and functions of Communes are of obvious interest to the leaders of the "Ujamaa" movement of Tanzania and the "Ejido" movement of Mexico. The emphasis on the use of local materials in intensive agriculture provides an important lesson for development planners. On a more fundamental level, the political and ideological bases of modern China grew from the experience of prolonged war and revolution. Such circumstances are unlikely to reoccur elsewhere in the absence of similar social upheavals; there are those who believe that a just society is impossible without such social disruption.

XIV   ACKNOWLEDGEMENTS

My thanks are due to the Commission on the Churches' Participation in Development, of the World Council of Churches, who, through the kind agency of Mr. Luis Carlos Weil, made possible the visit to China here described.

Thanks are also due to the officers of the Scotland China Association who arranged the visit and to fellow travellers, Radha Sinha, Johnathan Wills, Edith Wright, Alex Reid and Howard Wagstaff, who provided information included in this report. Radha Sinha provided much of the data in Annex 1 and, aided by Johnathan Wills, made most of the tape recordings used to supplement my notes. (The errors in transcription and note-taking are all mine).

I also wish to thank my colleague John Chinnery, of the Department of Chinese of the University of Edinburgh, for much help and guidance in things Chinese; he came to China but was incapacitated by illness for much of the visit. My colleague Iain Shepherd, of the School of Engineering Science of the University of Edinburgh, read earlier drafts of this report and eliminated some of my errors.

Last, but certainly not least I record my thanks to those citizens of the People's Republic of China whose paths I crossed and who made me welcome; perhaps I could add a special 'thank-you' to the pragmatic people of the Chengchow district of Honan province.

ANNEX 1

Some Social Indicators of present day China :

- figures relate to 1970 or later unless otherwise indicated

Population	*760×10^6
Land area	$9.6 \times 10^6 \ km^2$
Population density	79 inhabitants/km^2
Population density (main agricultural areas)	200 inhabitants/km^2
Urban population	14% of population
Literacy	40% of population
Primary school enrolment	95% of appropriate age groups
Persons per hospital bed (1959)	1800
Persons per 'Western' Doctor (1968)	7300
Persons per doctor, 'Western' and 'Traditional' (1968)	1250
Population, natural growth (1960's)	2.4 - 1.8% per annum
Population, natural growth (current)	1.4% per annum
Large city population, natural growth (current)	1.3% - 0.7% per annum

Per Capita Consumption :

Calories	2050 per day
Protein, animal and vegetable	57 gm. per day
Sugar	2 kg. per annum
Cotton piece goods	9 m^2 per annum
Radio receivers per 1000 of population	16

* Population figures are uncertain. Estimates range from
  680 to 820 millions. 'Western' observers tend to the higher
  figures. Recent census reports from China appear to confirm
  a figure of no more than 700 million. In this report 760
  million has been taken but it may well be 10% too great.

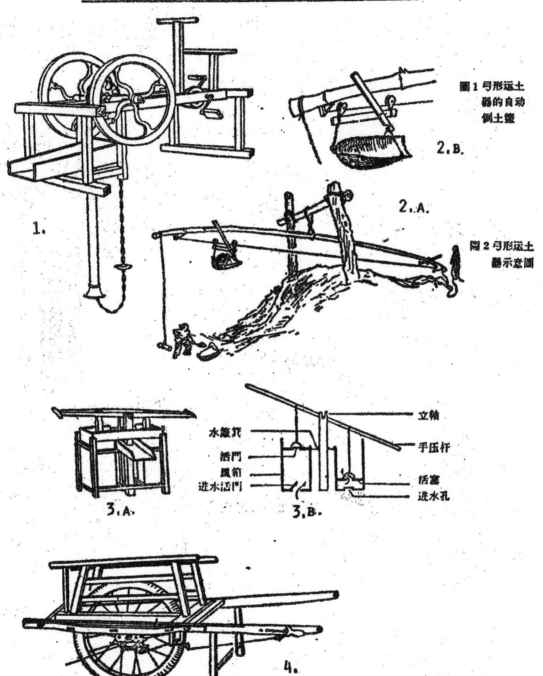

1.

圖1 弓形运土
器的自动
倒土箕

2.B.

2.A.

图2 弓形运土
器示意图

3.A.

3.B.

水箕筐
活門
風箱
进水活門

立軸
手压杆
活塞
进水孔

4.

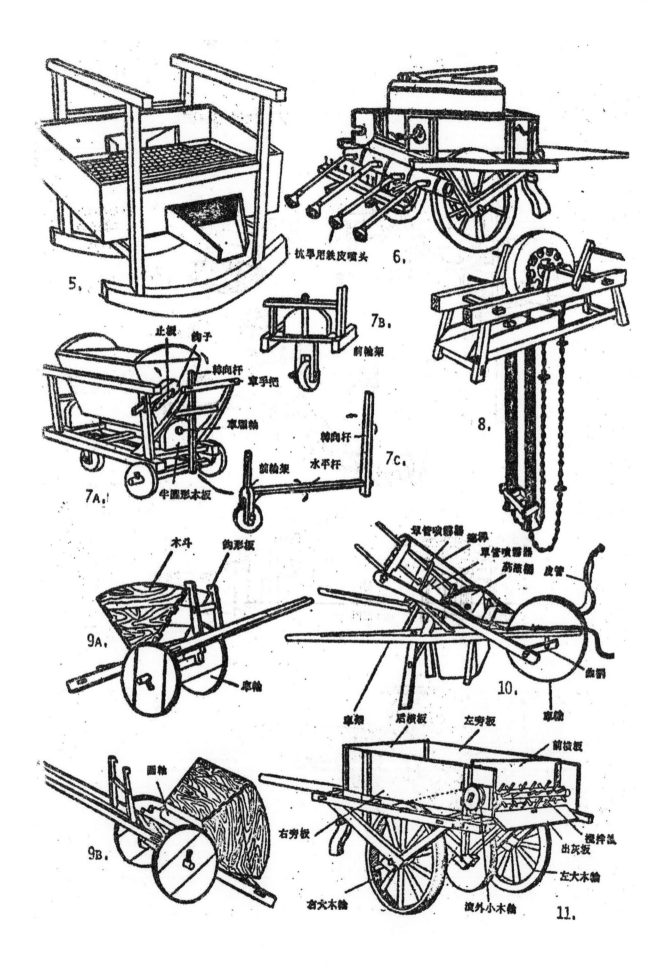

5.

6.

抗旱用鉄皮嘴头

7B. 前輪架

止板　鉤子
轉向杆
車手把
半圓形木板
車輪軸
7A.

7C. 轉向杆
前輪架　水平杆

8.

9A. 木斗　鉤形板
車輪

草管喷霧器　扳押
草管喷霧器
药瓶罐　皮管
曲弼
車輪

10.

9B. 圓軸

車輌　后横板　左芳板　前横板
右芳板
右大木輪
後外小木輪
左大木輪
攪拌艦
出灰板

11.

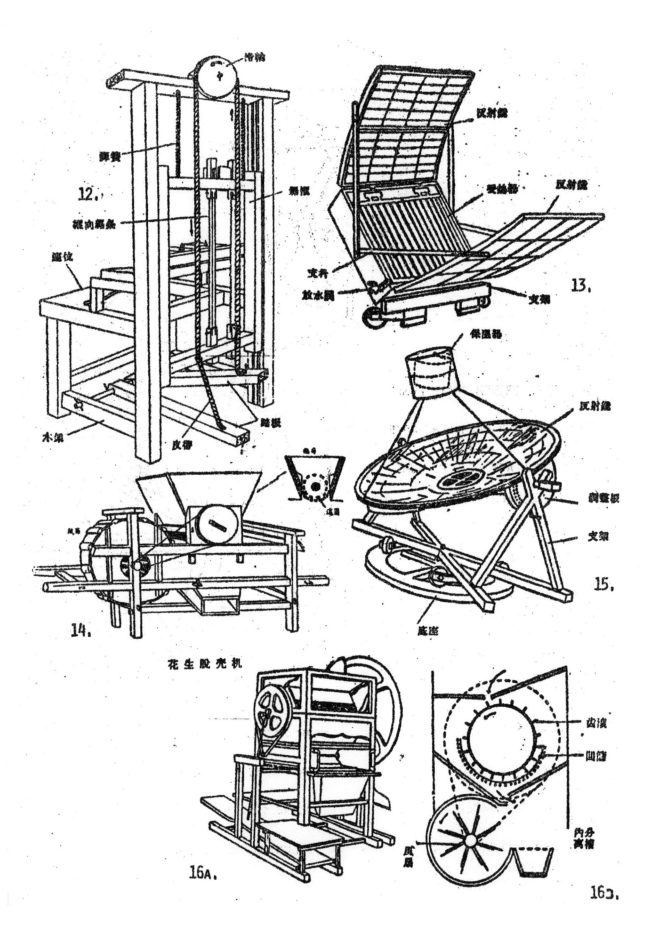

弹簧

滑轮

纵向锯条

机框

座位

木架

皮带

踏板

12.

反射镜

受热器

反射镜

支架

原料

放水阀

13.

保温器

反射镜

调整板

支架

底座

15.

风扇

14.

花生脱壳机

16A.

齿滚

凹槽

风扇

内分离槽

16B.

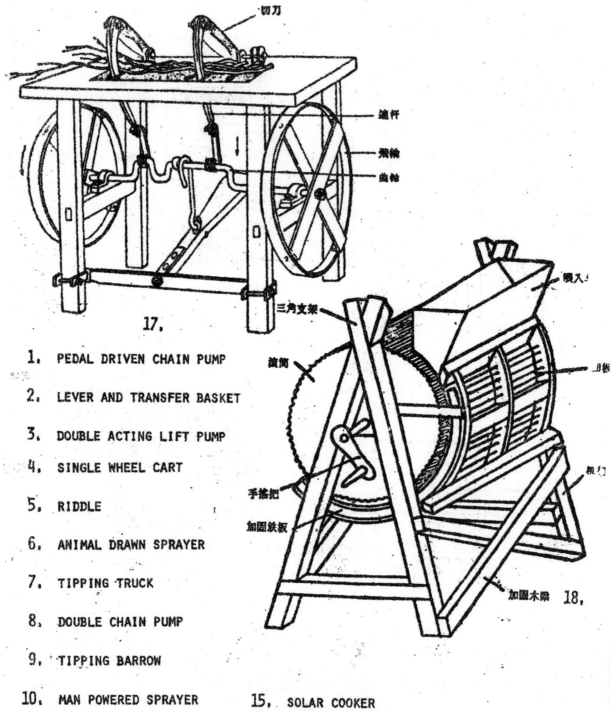

切刀

逼杆
飛輪
齒軸

三角支架

滾筒

頂入

月板

手搖把

加固鉄板

加固木梁

相?

17.

18.

1. PEDAL DRIVEN CHAIN PUMP

2. LEVER AND TRANSFER BASKET

3. DOUBLE ACTING LIFT PUMP

4. SINGLE WHEEL CART

5. RIDDLE

6. ANIMAL DRAWN SPRAYER

7. TIPPING TRUCK

8. DOUBLE CHAIN PUMP

9. TIPPING BARROW

10. MAN POWERED SPRAYER

11. MANURE SPREADER

12. PEDAL OPERATED SAW

13. SOLAR WATER HEATER

14. GROUNDNUT DE-HUSKER

15. SOLAR COOKER

16. GROUNDNUT DE-HUSKER

17. KINDLING CHOPPER

18. GROUNDNUT DE-HUSKER

DATA.

Paul

Cultivable land $1.07 \times 10^6 \text{ Km}^2$ (11% of total area)

——— $1.13 \times 10^6 \text{ Km}^2$ (11%) of wasteland which could be cultivated at a price. (Agrees with table in RC(1992)

Yellow River carries soil away at a rate of $3.7 \times 10^3 \text{ t/Km}^2$ on average each year (max^m (extreme?) $10 \times 10^3 \text{ t/Km}^2$) Each tonne of _loess_ contains 0.8 to 1.5 kg nitrates; 1.5 kg phosphates and 20 kg potassium

Printed by Amazon Italia Logistica S.r.l.
Torrazza Piemonte (TO), Italy